PARADOX

MARGARET CUONZO

W0006334

The MIT Press | Cambridge, Massachusetts | London, England

This book was set in Chaparral by the MIT Press. Printed and bound in the United States of America.

Library of Congress Cataloging-in-Publication Data

Cuonzo, Margaret, 1969–
Paradox / Margaret Cuonzo.
   pages   cm.—(MIT Press essential knowledge)
Includes bibliographical references and index.
ISBN 978-0-262-52549-7 (pbk. : alk. paper) 1. Paradox. 2. Intuition.
I. Title.
BC199.P2C86 2014
165—dc23
2013017733

10   9   8   7   6   5   4   3   2

For my favorite paradox solvers, my nephews
Anthony and Andrew

CONTENTS

SERIES FOREWORD

The MIT Press Essential Knowledge series offers accessible, concise, beautifully produced pocket-size books on topics of current interest. Written by leading thinkers, the books in this series deliver expert overviews of subjects that range from the cultural and the historical to the scientific and the technical.

In today's era of instant information gratification, we have ready access to opinions, rationalizations, and superficial descriptions. Much harder to come by is the foundational knowledge that informs a principled understanding of the world. Essential Knowledge books fill that need. Synthesizing specialized subject matter for nonspecialists and engaging critical topics through fundamentals, each of these compact volumes offers readers a point of access to complex ideas.

Bruce Tidor
Professor of Biological Engineering and Computer Science
Massachusetts Institute of Technology

PREFACE

When I began the long journey of writing this book almost fifteen years ago, I set out to write a treatise on famous paradoxes such as the liar paradox (which arises from the claim that *what I'm now claiming is false*). The plan was to expand on the treatment given in my dissertation of the sorites paradox, which concerns the precise number of grains of sand necessary for something to be classified as a heap. I imagined dividing the book into the major categories of paradoxes: the semantic, epistemic, logical, and so on, solving each with my preferred treatment. Along the way, though, a number of roadblocks, detours, and accidental discoveries occurred. The first was finding out that I needed to rethink the nature of paradox itself and that, coincidentally, a new way of thinking about belief being discussed in philosophy of science circles (and using subjective probability) was a useful way to do so. I also discovered that the standard views of the origins of paradox were misleading. I had thought of paradoxes as emerging in great part through Zeno of Elea, and their solutions with Aristotle, but both of these views were misrepresentations of a much longer tradition. And, most important, I found that the well-worn path of focusing on the paradoxes themselves wouldn't lead to anything nearly as original and interesting as focusing on the strategies for solving them. So, I switched course and I invite you to join me as I rethink the nature of paradoxes and, more important, the solutions that have been given to them. I hope to show you that although the standard attempts to solve the great puzzles of philosophy and other fields are often false starts leading to dead ends and that adopting a very minimalistic approach to paradoxes is most often the safest route to take, this limited "hands-off" approach is by no means a road to nowhere. There is much to be learned from the paradoxes and the types of the solution they admit, regardless of whether we can consider any of the more powerful paradoxes capable of solution.

The first impetus for setting out on this journey was a couple of brief passages in my former adviser Stephen Schiffer's works "Two Issues of Vagueness" (1999) and *The Things We Mean* (2003). Schiffer began to wonder about how successful any of the standard solutions to paradoxes were and created a division between what he called *happy-face* and *unhappy-face* solutions to paradoxes. Stephen Schiffer and his work have been key influences on this book and my philosophical thinking in general. Along the way, I was also privileged to attend a National Endowment for the Humanities summer seminar on error and statistical reasoning, organized by Deborah Mayo at Virginia Tech. This is where I first learned of Bayesianism and its use of subjective degrees of belief. And although Deborah convinced me of the limits of Bayesianism with respect to the confirmation and disconfirmation of scientific hypotheses, I found the Bayesian model quite useful in understanding paradoxes and why some paradoxes are more paradoxical than others. Other influences on this work include responses to papers that are incorporated into the chapters, especially those given at the Long Island Philosophical Society (LIPS), the organization I co-chaired with my friend James Friel. Anton Alterman and Glenn Statile provided useful critiques of the papers, and the book is much better for them. My colleague and friend Joseph Filonowicz, through his writing, teaching style, and general way of being, taught me to avoid worn out philosophical jargon and to experiment in my thinking and teaching. If this book gives pleasure to the general reader, it is due to Joe's insistence that philosophical rigor and accessibility are not mutually exclusive. I would also like to thank my wonderful colleagues Kristana Arp, Chris Araujo, Michael Pelias, Amy Robinson, Maksim Vak, Sophia Wong, and the other members of the Philosophy Department at Long Island University–Brooklyn, which I chaired for six years and currently co-chair. Also, the members of my beloved journal group, including writers Gerry Albarelli, Helen Duberstein, Joan Durant, Eva Kollisch, Edith Konecky, and Eva White, encouraged me to pay as much attention to having a good, clear narrative as to having interesting arguments. Writer and oral historian Gerry Albarelli and I held "retreats" in his house in Cambridge, Massachusetts, and critiqued each other's work. Having the input of someone who is a genius at hearing the story in even the most abstract of discussions and for questioning the "facts" that are laid down by an author was a great gift for which I am immensely grateful. Also, my dear friend, Dana Lerner, has tirelessly encouraged me for almost twenty years now. And my sweetheart, Vita Wallace, carefully edited this manuscript, delighted and soothed me with her musical and edible creations, and made the last few years of my life my happiest. I am also very grateful to the supremely competent and supportive Philip Laughlin at the MIT Press, who saw potential in the work and championed it. Three anonymous reviewers provided much needed and appreciated feedback, as well. Finally, my family continues to provide much encouragement and support in all my endeavors. The loving memory of my mother, Rosemarie Cuonzo, and the continued nagging (er, I mean cheerleading) of my father, Antonio Cuonzo, kept me on track through some challenging times. And my nephews Anthony and Andrew, with their love of paradoxes and puzzles, are always a source of joy and motivation. I hope that you, reader, derive as much pleasure and enrichment on this journey through solutions and their paradoxes as I have.

INTRODUCTION: IS THERE TROUBLE IN PARADOX?

In a BBC television series aptly called *Paradox*, a British astrophysicist claims to have images of a future explosion in which many people are going to die. After seeing these images of the future, poor harried detective Rebecca Flint must try to prevent this vision from coming to be. But if Flint is successful, then wouldn't the images of the "future" thus be false? If all the destruction predicted in the images of the future never came to be, even if it were thanks to Flint, in what sense could these images be thought reliable? The puzzling nature of time has given rise to many philosophical paradoxes. In addition to problems like Flint's, which are about altering the future based on our foreknowledge of it, there are also problems associated with the past, such as the grandfather paradox: the paradox associated with the question of whether it is conceptually possible to go back in time and kill your own grandfather before he met your grandmother. If it is indeed possible, then because you would not have existed in this scenario, it seems to be impossible. Because one of your parents would not have been born, you would not have been born, and hence you could not go back in time to kill your grandfather before he met your grandmother.

On a very broad construal, a *paradox* can be anything from a tough problem or a counterintuitive opinion or conclusion to a visual sleight of hand. An Internet search on the word *paradox*, for example, turns up the intricate and surprisingly beautiful prints of M. C. Escher; a picture of a glass ashtray with a "no smoking" symbol imprinted on it; a picture of a self-flowing flask, attributed to Robert Boyle, that is constantly refilling itself with the water that pours out from its base (figure 1); and a Wikipedia article listing more than two hundred paradoxes, including the grandfather paradox mentioned earlier. The paradoxes listed come from such diverse areas as statistics, thermodynamics, economics, biology, and logic. What, then, makes them all paradoxes?

Philosophers are by no means in complete agreement about the correct way to define *paradox*, but each of the prominent definitions points to an important feature of paradox. One common definition (Rescher 2001) holds that a *paradox* is *a set of mutually inconsistent propositions, each of which seems true*. Consider Flint's problem of trying to prevent an event in the future from happening. There are a number of propositions—let's call them

On a very broad construal, a *paradox* can be anything from a tough problem or a counterintuitive opinion or conclusion to a visual sleight of hand.

Figure 1   Boyle's self-flowing flask
Image taken from Wikimedia commons. Also on http://www.lhup
.edu/~dsimanek/museum/people/people.htm.

statements—associated with her situation. First, assume that the images of the future explosion are reliable predictors of what will happen. Second, if this is the case, then nothing Flint does would seem to be able to alter what would happen, because we've assumed that they are correct. But, third, Flint seems to have the freedom to act in ways that would prevent the future explosion from happening. So, fourth, if Flint does succeed in preventing the explosion from happening, then the images of the future explosion were not accurate. Notice that the fourth statement contradicts the first one, which was taken as an assumption. If the pictures are reliable, then nothing can be done about the explosion. But because Flint is free to act as she chooses, she can do things that would prevent the explosion. However, if this is the case, then the pictures did not accurately predict the future. Each statement, in and of itself, looks acceptable, yet when put together, we have a contradiction:

Box 1

Flint's paradox

1. The pictures of the future explosion are accurate (assumption).
2. Nothing Flint can do can prevent the explosion (follows from 1).

Box 1 (continued)

3. Flint has the freedom to behave in ways that would prevent the explosion.
4. The pictures of the future explosion may turn out to not be accurate (from 3; contradicts 1).

This example illustrates that paradoxes involve some type of contradiction among claims that, at least on the surface, have nothing wrong with them. Perhaps this is why an Internet search for *paradox* turns up a picture of an ashtray with a "no smoking" symbol inscribed on it. Individually, the ashtray and the symbol are perfectly common items in our environment. Yet by putting them together in one object, a tension arises between an object that was created with the idea that smoking would happen and a sign that prohibits smoking from happening. In both the ashtray and in the grandfather paradox, the inconsistency is highlighted, along with the fact that no one member of the inconsistent set of assumptions is obviously wrong. An inconsistency among seemingly innocuous elements is thus central to the idea of paradox.

Other definitions highlight the reasoning involved in paradoxes. For example, some claim that a *paradox* is *an argument with seemingly valid reasoning and true premises, but an obviously false conclusion* (Mackie 1973) and still others claim that *paradoxes* are *unacceptable conclusions drawn from seemingly true premises and correct reasoning* (Sainsbury 2009). Arguments are pieces of reasoning in which one claim (the conclusion) is supported by other claims (the premises). When the reasoning is correct, true premises will always lead to true conclusions. But, in the case of paradoxes, it seems that something has gone wrong, in that true premises and correct reasoning lead to an obviously false or contradictory conclusion. In the Flint case, for example, we assumed that images of the future explosion were correct, but then concluded that if she had prevented the explosion from happening, then the images could not have been correct. So, we've concluded something that contradicts what we took as a given. Also, consider the sorites paradox, an early and famous paradox about vagueness that shows, it seems, that when there are no sharp boundaries between concepts such as *bald* and *non-bald* or *rich* and *not rich*, we can conclude some obviously false things. The sorites can be put in the form of the following argument:

Box 2

Sorites paradox

1. A person with 0 hairs is bald.
2. For any number n, if a person with n hairs is bald, then a person with $(n + 1)$ hairs is bald.

Box 2 (continued)

> 3. Therefore, a person with 1,000,000 hairs is bald.

In the sorites paradox, (1) and (2) are premises and (3) is the conclusion of the argument. The first premise, which claims that a person with zero hairs is bald, describes the paradigm case of baldness. Such a premise looks obviously true, because if any person were to be bald, the person with the fewest possible hairs (0) would be. The second premise, though perhaps difficult to read at first, is very intuitive as well. It claims that the difference of one hair is not enough to warrant the change in classification from being bald to being non-bald. If you add one hair to any person's head, in other words, it won't change whether that person is bald. Given that the difference of one hair is hardly noticeable by the human eye, it is hard to imagine how any kind of principled distinction between baldness and non-baldness could be made based on one hair. With regard to its reasoning, the sorites is straightforward. The first premise claims that a person with a specific number of hairs (0) is bald. The second premise makes a claim about all numbers of hairs, saying that for any arbitrary number, one more would not make enough of a difference to warrant a change in classification from someone being bald

bald to non-bald. The number used in the first premise (0) is plugged into the generalization in the second premise, repeatedly, to get the conclusion that a person with a million hairs is bald. So, phrased in this way, the sorites paradox is an argument with intuitively plausible premises, apparently correct reasoning, and an obviously false or contradictory conclusion. It can also be thought of, using Mark Sainsbury's definition, as an unacceptable conclusion ("A person with 1,000,000 hairs is bald") that is derived from apparently acceptable premises ("A person with 0 hairs is bald," and "For any number n, if a person with n hairs is bald, a person with $(n + 1)$ hairs is bald"), using apparently correct reasoning. These two definitions therefore highlight another important feature of paradoxes,[1] namely, how the use of seemingly fine premises and seemingly good reasoning sometimes turns up unexpectedly strange conclusions.

Paradoxes expose some kind of trouble with our reasoning, or the statements we take as premises, or the basic concepts that underlie the paradox in question. In Flint's case, the trouble the paradox exposes is whether foreknowledge of the future (that the images of the future explosion gave) means that the future is already predetermined. In the sorites paradox, it is troubling that vague terms like *bald*, *strong*, and *rich* have to apply to some things and not others, but saying precisely how few hairs makes someone bald, how much weight lifted makes something strong, or

Paradoxes expose
some kind of trouble
with our reasoning, or
the statements we
take as premises, or the
basic concepts that
underlie the paradox
in question.

how many pennies one must have to count as rich doesn't make much sense. We have to admit that there is a difference between being bald and not bald, but no specific number of hairs would be a good boundary to mark that difference. And the same goes for weight and strength, and pennies and wealth. It is this type of trouble that leads us to want to figure out what has gone awry in the paradox.

Presenting solutions to paradoxes, generating new paradoxes, and criticizing proposed solutions to paradoxes are all part of the workaday life of philosophers, theoretical physicists, economists, and other theoreticians. From the very brief introduction to the Flint, the grandfather, and the sorites paradoxes, possible solutions may have begun spontaneously emerging in your mind. For example, in the case of Flint's paradox, you might think it shows that there can be no correct images of the future. Or perhaps you thought that the paradox showed that the future must be predetermined, and there was nothing Flint could do to stop the explosion. Or both. And perhaps you started thinking that the grandfather paradox shows that there can be no time travel.

Proposing solutions is a natural response to paradoxes and is probably as old as philosophy itself. Very early in the Western philosophical tradition, Aristotle—the philosopher often called the "father" of systematic logic—studied and attempted to solve paradoxes. For him, paradoxes were flawed arguments, and to solve a paradox was to point to the flaw in the argument (Kneale and Kneale 1962). Some of his main targets were the paradoxes of Zeno of Elea, whose arguments on space, time, and motion are thought to be the earliest paradoxes in the Western philosophical tradition. And the generation of paradoxes and solutions continues until the present day. As shown in the final chapter of this book, the process of paradox generation and solution proposal is an interesting and important one. New sciences often stem from attempts to solve paradoxes, and the concepts used in the new sciences lead to further paradoxes.

One common misconception that I hope will be shown to be mistaken is that paradoxes are puzzles that—although they are interesting—remain removed from everyday life. Nothing could be further from the truth. Paradoxes emerge in everyday sources, in the newspapers, in religious texts, in conversations, and in practical dilemmas that must be faced in one's life. To give an example, during the writing of this book, an article in the *Wall Street Journal* discussed Santon Bridge, a small English town that hosts an annual World's Biggest Liar Competition (MacDonald 2011). The town must be awash in paradox.

Also, it will soon become apparent that the solutions to paradoxes have implications in other aspects of our lives. Fuzzy logic, for example, with its use of degrees of truth, underlies such mundane but useful things as signature recognition programs. Without a method of dealing with the

Paradoxes emerge in everyday sources, in the newspapers, in religious texts, in conversations, and in practical dilemmas that must be faced in one's life.

borderline cases between, say, a handwritten *a* and a handwritten *u*, such programs would not be possible. And without decision theory, public policy would be handicapped. Solutions and their paradoxes, then, are important parts of the world in which we live.

This idea was brought home to me when I was in the British Library about ten years ago and found a dusty volume that contained the Conway Memorial Lecture given by J. C. Flugel to a London ethical society in 1941 at the height of World War II. The address began, "This is the sixth Conway Memorial Lecture (out of a total series of thirty-two) to be delivered during war; and since a year ago . . . war has come very appreciably nearer to our doors, so near indeed, that we may count ourselves fortunate if Conway Hall still stands, and we ourselves still free to meet within it; for we know that at any moment actual combat, with its noisy and destructive clamor, may break out around us, threatening our lives, the lives of those who are near and dear to us, and the works and monuments of those who lived here before us and established the traditions that we are seeking to maintain" (Flugel 1941, 1). Upon reading this, I thought, "Why on Earth were these people gathered in downtown London to listen to a lecture while bombs might fall down upon them?" The lecture must have been about something very important to the members of the audience at that time. Flugel continued, "At such times it is difficult or impossible to divert our thoughts for long from the tremendous conflict going on around us, and I have made no attempt to do so in this lecture" (1).

The subject that had brought out the attendees and speaker was the paradoxical nature of war—in particular, how something as obviously immoral as war could induce in the belligerent groups such impressive moral qualities as self-sacrifice and generosity toward one's fellows. In the lecture, which was titled "The Moral Paradox of Peace and War," Flugel questioned why war, though terribly destructive, induces a higher moral state within particular groups. This issue was a paradox that those in attendance were experiencing directly, and one that must have inspired the audience to attend a lecture at such a time. A number of responses to the paradox suggest themselves, such as that the supposed conflict between war being a horrible thing and it being the inspiration for benevolent and even heroic acts is nonexistent. Both can exist without much conflict at all. This is what I describe later as an It's-All-Good response. But the point brought home by those people gathered at Conway Hall in 1941 London is even more profound than the paradox they discussed—namely, that paradoxes are important to humans, because they highlight conflicts between some of the beliefs we hold most dear. By bringing to light conflicts among our firmly held beliefs, paradoxes demand answers from us. If we are to lead lives guided by reason, we must respond to the paradoxes that arise among the beliefs we take to be true. This is why,

I believe, it was perfectly understandable to forego other obligations to attend such a lecture at that very tense time. And it is why, in our pursuit of paradoxes and solutions, we are engaged in more than mere puzzle solving. We are committing ourselves to lives that are more thoughtful and better guided by reason.

In the following chapters, we will look at new ways of thinking about paradoxes (chapter 1), how they are generated (chapter 2), and also how they are best solved (chapter 3). The glossary of key terms provides further explanation for the general reader. There is, I hope, insight into the nature of paradoxes and enjoyment in considering their proposed solutions in much of what follows.

A NEW WAY TO THINK ABOUT PARADOXES AND SOLUTIONS

1.1 Introduction: The Intuitive Basis of Paradox

We have already discussed three ways of defining *paradox*, namely as (1) *a set of inconsistent statements, in which each statement seems true* (Rescher 2001), (2) *an argument with seemingly good assumptions, seemingly fine reasoning, but an obviously false conclusion* (Mackie 1973), and (3) *an unacceptable conclusion derived from seemingly good premises using seemingly good reasoning* (Sainsbury 2009). Notice how many times the words *seems* or *seemingly* appear in each of these definitions. Even with the broadest construal of the word *paradox*, which includes images and the like, paradoxes involve conflicts among seemingly unproblematic elements. Paradoxes force us to rethink the way things seem to us, because they expose two or more common-sense beliefs that contradict each other and suggest that seemingly perfectly good reasoning can lead us to contradiction or obvious falsity. In other words, paradoxes force us to question whether our intuitive understanding of the world is really accurate. The term *paradox* comes from the ancient Greek terms for *against* or *beyond* (*para*, παρά) and *expectation* or *opinion* (*doxa*, δόξα). The Greek terms emphasize the counterintuitive nature of paradoxes. Our intuitions about the world, then, are central to what it means to be a paradox.

Take, for example, a problem from biology called "the paradox of enrichment." Intuitively, one would think that a population of predators would tend to do better if the amount of food available to its prey were to increase. More food for the prey means that more prey is available to the predator, and hence the predators' population should expand as well. Yet, in fact, sometimes the opposite happens (Rosensweig 1971). An increase in the food available to rabbits, for example, in a given area might lead to an overabundance of rabbits, and increase the population of its predator—say, wolves—until the population of wolves becomes unsustainably large and is destabilized. So, more food for the rabbits can actually pose a threat to the population of wolves. This example shows that our ordinary intuition—that more food and hence more prey is always good for a predatory group—is flawed. More is not always more, at least in the case of predators and prey. The paradox of enrichment shows that our intuitions about

Paradoxes force us to question whether our intuitive understanding of the world is really accurate.

abundance and enrichment do not always conform to observable facts.[1]

In the paradox of enrichment, an assumption that we took to be intuitively plausible turned out, along with other evidence, to lead to unexpected conclusions. For this reason, our intuitions about what is good for a population of animals had to be questioned and, as a result, progress was made in the form of new models of predator/prey relations (May 1972). So, by questioning our most basic intuitions, we are often led to new ways about thinking about our basic notions and, ironically, to further paradoxes.

Intuition has been variously defined as *seeming truth*, *spontaneous mental judgment*, *what we would say* in a given situation, and *noninferential belief* (Davis-Floyd and Arvidson 1997). And, more recently, it has been described by cognitive scientists as immediate judgments that arise from the recognition of familiar elements in a new situation (Kahneman 2011). It is intuitively obvious to me right now that I am typing on a laptop computer, that murder is immoral, that triangles have three sides, that the gray and tan object poking out from behind the computer screen is Coco the cat, and so on. In addition, my beliefs about these things were fairly immediate. I didn't need to infer any of these beliefs from a set of assumptions. They came to me spontaneously and without forethought. But giving an account of intuitiveness is not an easy endeavor. If there were a way not only to explain the intuitiveness of the components of the paradox but also to quantify the degree to which a part of a paradox is intuitive, we would have a better understanding of the nature of paradox.

1.2   Enter Subjective Probability: The Degree to Which We Believe Things

Recently, a new way of thinking about belief emerged in the philosophy of science that can give us a better understanding of the intuitive nature of paradox. A group of philosophers of science known as *Bayesians* started to use something called *subjective probability* to explain the degree to which a scientific hypothesis is confirmed or disconfirmed. Subjective probability is the degree to which a rational observer believes something, with 0 assigned to complete disbelief, 1 to complete certainty, 0.5 for neither belief nor disbelief, 0.7 for fairly strong belief, and so on (see table 1).

Thinking in terms of degrees of belief makes sense, especially when we are dealing with uncertainty about the future. Right now, for example, I believe that a gift I just ordered online will arrive in time for me to present it my friend on her birthday. I am, however, not completely certain about this. Because the online store usually delivers things in a timely fashion, I'm pretty sure it will arrive in time. But I did not opt for a guaranteed delivery date, so

Table 1 Sample degrees of belief for one rational believer

Degree of belief	Sample belief
0.0	Belief that 2 + 2 = 5
0.1	Belief that meat consumption is morally acceptable
0.2	Belief that God exists
0.3	Belief that environmental damage can still be completely reversed
0.4	Belief that my dog will live to 18 years of age
0.5	Belief that the results of the next coin toss will be heads
0.6	Belief that the U.S. economy is improving
0.7	Belief that Hillary Clinton will win the next presidential election
0.8	Belief that in five years most books will be digitized
0.9	Belief that smoking is bad for one's health
1.0	Belief that 2 + 2 = 4

I'm taking my chances. Given what I know about the store, the mail service, the doormen who work in my friend's building, and so on, my subjective probability that the gift will arrive on time is about 0.8. But this number could be revised up or down, depending on a number of factors. If, for example, a terrible storm hits the region, then my subjective probability would drop, and if I received an email saying the item was shipped yesterday, my subjective probability would rise. The degrees to which we believe things get raised or lowered, then, depending on the evidence we have available to us. And when the birthday comes, my degree of belief will be raised either to 1, complete belief, or lowered to 0, complete disbelief. I will know whether it has arrived in time.

Although it is called *subjective probability*, subjective probability is not a totally subjective measure, because it assumes that the believer is rational. As Richard Jeffrey has written (2004, 76), "Your 'subjective' probability is not something fetched out of the sky on a whim; it is what your judgment *should* be in view of your information to date, and of your sense of other people's information, even if you do not regard it as a judgment that everyone must share on pain of being wrong in one sense or another." Although there might be some leeway with regard to the degrees of rational belief, believers are constrained by rules of rationality and the information available to them. For example, a rational believer would not have a subjective probability of 1 for a contradictory proposition. Nor would such a believer assign a contradiction a probability of 0.6. Though I doubt people go through their daily lives assigning numerical probabilities to partial beliefs, when asked how sure they are about something, people can in general say whether they think something is more likely than not (greater than 0.5), almost certain (0.9), or similar estimates.

Using subjective probability, we can give an account of the intuitiveness of the parts of any paradox—even for the intuitiveness of a paradox as a whole. The more intuitive a statement in a paradox is, the higher its subjective probability is. And when we get contradictory conclusions, we know that that part of the paradox must have a subjective probability of 0. In the case of the deepest paradoxes, we have premises with extremely high subjective probabilities and a conclusion that is accorded 0—or just slightly above it. So, we can rate how deep a paradox is by using subjective probability. To see how this can happen, let's examine how different subjective probabilities are combined.

If I believe strongly that the gift I ordered for my friend will arrive in time for her birthday (0.8) and very strongly that my friend will like the gift (0.9), then the subjective probability that both of these things will happen is the combined subjectivity of both beliefs. Because it is less likely for both to happen than for one to happen individually, the combined subjective probability of the two beliefs would be slightly lower than each, and best calculated by multiplying the two degrees of probability.[2] If I multiply the two numbers (0.9 and 0.8), I get 0.72. So I think my chances of my gift being received and appreciated are pretty good. Why multiplication? We need to allow for how some uncertainty in individual beliefs combine to form even greater uncertainty in combined beliefs. If I believe something with a subjective probability of 0.2 and another with 0.9, then my subjective probability about both being the case should be quite low, given the low belief I have

Using subjective prob-
ability, we can give an
account of the intuitive-
ness of the parts of
any paradox—even for
the intuitiveness of a
paradox as a whole.

about one of them. And multiplication models this effect for us. Under this way of thinking about degrees of belief, the result would be 0.18—a small bit lower than 0.2, because when we combine a very low subjective probability (0.2) with something less than complete subjective certainty, such as a 0.9 belief, then the 0.2 belief should be lowered to account for the added amount of uncertainty.

1.3   Using Subjective Probability to Analyze Paradoxes

Paradoxes, by the second definition mentioned in the first paragraph of this chapter, involve *seemingly* true assumptions and *apparently* correct reasoning. The intuitiveness of each part of a paradox and the depth of a paradox as a whole can be given using subjective probability.

To do this, let's introduce what I'll call a *paradoxicality rating* for paradoxes modeled, to start, on the definition of a *paradox* as an argument with seemingly true premises, seemingly valid[3] reasoning, and an obviously false or contradictory conclusion. The paradoxicality rating of an argument would then be determined by combining (a) the subjective probability of the conjunction of the premises $Pr(p1, \ldots, pn)$ being true, (b) the subjective probability of valid (Prv) reasoning, and (c) the subjective probability of a false conclusion c, or $(1 - Prc)$. Thus we get the formula, which is really just one long multiplication of the subjective probabilities of the parts of a paradox, where Pr stands for subjective probability, p for the premises, v for the validity of the reasoning, and c for the conclusion:

Box 3

Paradoxicality rating

Paradoxicality = $\Pr(p1, \ldots, pn) \times \Pr v \times (1 - \Pr c)$

Because paradoxes on this first definition are arguments, we need to factor in the subjective probabilities of all the parts of the paradoxical argument, including the subjective probabilities of the premises, that the reasoning is good, and that the conclusion is false. The higher the subjective probability of a premise, the more likely we are to bet that this premise is true, and the more "intuitive strength" the premise will have for us. With the probability of the conclusion and the argument's validity held constant, the higher the subjective probability of a premise, the higher the degree to which an argument is paradoxical. For example, if we have an argument with a clearly false premise, it doesn't pose much of a paradox for us, because we never found the premise to be intuitively plausible to begin with. If we never really thought that more food for prey would translate into more prey and hence a better situation for the predator, for example, we wouldn't find the paradox of enrichment very deep or paradoxical at all. It is because we *do* think more food for prey means more prey and hence a better situation for predators that the conflicting evidence seems surprising and paradoxical, which is why, in the definition of paradoxicality, we do a straightforward multiplication of the subjective probabilities of the premises, $\Pr(p1, \ldots, pn)$.

As for the reasoning involved, the more obvious it seems that the reasoning is good, the deeper the paradox becomes. For example, consider Rebecca Flint and her problems with the images of the future explosion. It does seem quite clear that if the assumption that the images presented to Flint are veridical is given, and we assume she has free will, we can use very straightforward reasoning to derive a contradiction. If the images are true, then the explosion will happen, but if Flint is free, she can prevent the explosion from happening. So, given the premises that (1) the images of the future explosion are true, which we assume and (2) Flint is free to prevent future events from happening, we are licensed to conclude that Flint cannot change the future (from 1) and yet can change the future (from 2). And this conclusion is a contradiction. It is an example of seemingly good reasoning. The more straightforward the reasoning is in an argument, the higher the degree to which the argument is paradoxical. If we knew, for example, that a logical fallacy (i.e., an error in reasoning) was used in the argument, then the argument would not be very deep or paradoxical. Real paradoxes, by this definition, are arguments for which the reasoning is straightforwardly correct. The more obviously correct the reasoning is, the more paradoxical the argument.

The final item to be factored in is the subjective probability that the conclusion is false. In the previous Flint paradox example, we derived a contradiction. Contradictions always get a subjective probability of 0. If the conclusion were probably true, then we wouldn't think that the argument was very paradoxical. If we accepted the conclusion that a person with 1,000,000 hairs is bald, for example, we wouldn't find the sorites paradox very deep. The problem, though, is that we *do* think the conclusion is false—and even if we didn't, we could posit an even higher number of hairs as meeting the requirement for baldness. So, with other factors held constant, the lower the subjective probability of the conclusion, the more paradoxical the argument is. If you look at the formula in box 3, though, you'll see that although I'm doing a straight multiplication of probabilities, the conclusion's probability is subtracted from 1. The reason we have the $(1 - Prc)$ at the end of the definition is that we don't want to factor in how high the subjective probability of the conclusion is, but instead how low it is. And subtracting the subjective probability of the conclusion from 1 lets us do this.

The more straight-forward the reasoning is in an argument, the higher the degree to which the argument is paradoxical.

So that you can learn how to use the formula for paradoxicality to determine how intuitively plausible a paradox is, let's look at a few cases. In an argument with two premises, each with a subjective probability of 0.5, the premises would have a combined probability of 0.25. If the reasoning is unquestionably valid, then we can give the argument a Prv value of 1, and if the conclusion is highly unlikely—say, 0.2—then 1 – Prc is 0.8. The total paradoxicality rating is $0.25 \times 1 \times 0.8 = 0.2$, which is not very high, because the premises were not very likely.

If you have an argument like the sorites paradox discussed in the introduction, then you have an argument with extremely plausible premises. The first premise—that a person with no hair on his head is bald—is close to a conceptual truth and deserves a probability of 1. The second premise, which says that adding 1 hair won't make a difference regarding whether someone is bald, is seemingly conceptual as well, but perhaps there is a bit more room for doubt with this premise. I would give this premise a 0.95. The reasoning is straightforward, and Prv would be 1. The conclusion that a person with 1,000,000 hairs is bald is almost conceptually false and can be increased indefinitely. Thus Prc should be 0, and 1 – 0 is 1. So we have $1 \times 0.95 \times 1 \times (1 - 0) = 0.95$. Taken together, we have an argument with a paradoxicality rating of 0.95, a very high paradoxicality rating. On this way of ranking paradoxes, the sorites turns out to be quite paradoxical.

Not all arguments, of course, get such a high paradoxicality rating. Consider an argument known to be sound. By definition, a sound argument's premises are true, its reasoning valid, and its conclusion true. So the premises of such an argument have a combined subjective probability of 1, a subjective probability of its validity of 1, and a subjective probability of its conclusion of 1. A sound argument's paradoxicality rating is always 0, because of the conclusion. The conclusion has a subjective probability of 1 and the paradoxicality rating is determined by the formula $\Pr(p1, \ldots, pn) \times \Pr v \times (1 - \Pr c)$. Thus we have $1 \times 1 \times 0$, which assigns to a sound argument a paradoxicality rating of 0. Not only sound arguments, but all arguments with clearly true conclusions receive paradoxicality ratings of 0. An argument with a clearly true conclusion is nonparadoxical on any plausible definition and would therefore receive a paradoxicality rating of 0. In addition, arguments must not have obviously false premises to count as paradoxes. If the subjective probability of a premise is 0, then—regardless of the subjective probabilities of the conclusion and validity—the argument has a paradoxicality rating of 0.

By using the paradoxicality rating, we can distinguish between obviously nonparadoxical arguments, such as sound arguments and arguments with obviously false premises, and clear cases of paradoxicality. However, as you'll soon see, it would be unwise to give a set number for distinguishing the paradoxical from the nonparadoxical. Indeed, to do so would lead to further paradoxes. The paradoxicality rating determines what is more paradoxical than something else and identifies the very clear cases. As for the borderline cases of paradoxicality—for example, arguments in the 0.5 or 0.6 range—a paradoxicality rating merely points to the borderline nature of the paradox and distinguishes it from more clear cases.

So far, we have assumed the definition of *paradox* on which a paradox is an argument. If we think of a *paradox* as a set of mutually inconsistent statements, each of which seems true, we can give an alternative formula for determining how intuitive a paradox is. This formula combines the subjective probability of each of the statements, along with the subjective probability that the statements are inconsistent. We can symbolize this as follows, where Pr again represents subjective probability, each s refers to a statement in the set, and i represents the claim that the set of statements is inconsistent:

Box 4

Paradoxicality for sets of statements

Paradoxicality = $Pr(s1, s2, \ldots, sn) \times Pr(i)$

In other words, paradoxicality is determined by how high the subjective probability of each statement is, along with the probability that the set of statements is inconsistent.

For example, consider another paradox: the basic liar paradox. If we consider the statement (L), "This sentence is false," we see that if the statement (L) is true, then it is true that the statement is false, because the sentence claims that it is false. And if (L) is false, then it is false that the statement (L) is false, so the statement is true. So, if (L) is true, then it is false. And if (L) is false, then it is true. But because statements are either true or false, then it seems to follow that the statement would have to be both true and false, which is a contradiction. So we have a set of statements:

Box 5

Basic liar paradox

1. If L is true, then L is false.
2. If L is false, then L is true.
3. L is either true or false, but not both.

Each of these statements has a high subjective probability, given what L states. Yet all three cannot be true at the same time without contradiction, because the truth of L leads to its being false, and its falsity leads to its truth. And this contradiction violates statement 3, which claims that L cannot be both true and false. So we have three statements with high subjective probability and, taken as a set, they are inconsistent. When we plug very high values into the formula, $\Pr(1 \times 1 \times 0.9) \times \Pr(1)$, we get a paradox with a paradoxicality rating of 0.9, a very high rating. This result makes sense given that this paradox is considered one of deepest philosophical paradoxes.

As shown earlier, the paradoxicality rating can be used to assess the degree to which an argument is paradoxical. It also gives us a way of explaining why something is more paradoxical than something else. Consider the basic liar paradox and a strengthened version of the paradox. This next, stronger version of the paradox is more paradoxical because it makes an assumption that is harder to call into question. Because the basic liar sentence "This sentence is false" predicates falsity of itself, it is false in the event that it is true, and true in the event that it is false. Yet according to a basic rule called the principle of *bivalence* (the claim that every statement is either true or false), all propositions are either true or false. So regardless of which truth-value (true or false) is assigned to the sentence, the other one will automatically be assigned to it as well. Thus, it will be assigned both truth-values.

The only difference between the basic liar paradox just mentioned and the strengthened liar paradox is that the strengthened liar sentence is "This sentence is not true." If you abandon bivalence, you can solve the simple liar paradox, holding that the sentence is neither true nor false. However, the strengthened liar paradox assumes only the law of excluded middle, which claims that every statement or its denial is true. The principle of bivalence can, with some explanation, be denied, whereas it is far harder to deny a logical principle such as the law of excluded middle without leading to contradiction. So although someone might argue that the basic liar sentence is neither true nor false but meaningless, it would be much harder to apply the same treatment to the strengthened liar sentence. Doing so entails denying that the sentence is neither true nor untrue. In the first case, we could say that denying the truth of "This sentence is false" doesn't lead to the sentence being false, as the sentence could be meaningless or otherwise ill formed. In the second case, if we say that it's not the case that "This sentence is not true" is true, we seemingly *are* saying that it *is true*.

Thus, the strengthened liar paradox must have a higher paradoxicality rating than the basic liar paradox. Assume that all other parts of the liar and strengthened liar paradoxes are unquestionable—that is, the other premises are assigned subjective probabilities of 1 and the validity of each paradox is assigned 1—and that both conclusions are obviously false; hence $1 - \mathrm{Pr}c$ is $1 - 0$, or 1. In this case, the only difference between the two paradoxes in terms of their paradoxicality rating is due to the subjective probabilities of the basic liar sentence and the strengthened liar sentence. If, for example, the basic liar sentence is assigned a subjective probability of 0.90 and the strengthened liar sentence is assigned 0.95, then the strengthened liar sentence will have a paradoxicality rating of 0.95 and the basic liar sentence will have only a 0.90 rating. The strengthened liar statement will turn out to be just as paradoxical as the sorites paradox, but both the sorites and strengthened liar statements will be more paradoxical than the basic liar paradox.

Thus, when we make the idea of intuition more explicit by thinking of it in terms of subjective probability, we can explain why some things are more paradoxical than others. The paradoxicality rating gives us a way to do this. The liar paradox, in both its basic and strengthened versions, turns out to be more paradoxical than the paradox of enrichment, because both versions of the liar paradox have parts with high subjective probability. By contrast, the conclusion of the paradox of enrichment, though surprising, still has a lower probability than the parts of either paradox. So this paradox turns out to be less paradoxical (see table 2).

1.4   Subjective Probability and Solutions to Paradoxes

Solutions can also be explained in terms of the subjective probability of the parts of the paradox. There are many

Table 2 Sample list of paradoxes and approximate paradoxicality ratings

Paradox	Paradoxicality rating
Enrichment	0.07
Liar, basic	0.90
Liar, strengthened	0.95
Sorites	0.95

ways to solve paradoxes, but most involve pointing to one part of the paradox and lowering its subjective probability. For example, many philosophers have tried to solve the sorites paradox by showing that the premise that states that adding one hair won't make the difference in someone's being bald or non-bald (for any number n, if a person with n hairs on his head is bald, then a person with $n + 1$ hairs on his head is bald) is either false or very misleading.

Would-be solvers of the sorites paradox often try to show that this premise (which is sometimes called the *inductive premise*) is not true, and that one hair does make this difference. Timothy Williamson (1994), for example, argues that the principle of bivalence—which states that every statement is either true or false—is a true principle, and that because of this, in a series of hairs ranging from zero to a million, there must be a point in which one hair marks a shift from being bald to being non-bald. Once we reach that number—let's call it n—the statement "A person with n hairs is bald" would be true, and the statement "A person with $n + 1$ hairs is bald" false. This claim follows, Williamson thinks, from the premise that every statement is either true or false. Williamson's project is to show how this could be, and why our intuitions about the truth of the claim that the addition of one hair won't change anyone's status as bald are mistaken. To try to lower our subjective probability about this part of the paradox, Williamson says that it only seems like one hair wouldn't make a difference in whether someone is bald because we cannot know that point. Just because we are unable, due to our own limited abilities, to tell where the shift in numbers of hairs is, it doesn't follow that shift isn't there. In fact, the principle of bivalence shows that this shift must be there. In other words, we confuse our ignorance of the cutoff between baldness and non-baldness with the fact that there is no cutoff. If Williamson succeeded in this project, then the subjective probability of the second premise in the sorites paradox would be lowered.

Whether Williamson was successful is another matter. The point, though, is that his treatment of the paradox involved pointing to part of it and then trying to lower this part's subjective probability, showing how we were mistaken in giving that part of the paradox a high subjective probability.

For another example, consider Flint's problem of preventing the future explosion that was known to be coming. We saw that there was a conflict regarding how it is possible both for the images of the future explosion to be accurate and for it to be possible for Flint to stop the future explosion. One way to attempt to solve this paradox would be to claim that although it looks plausible that Flint has the power to prevent the future explosion, if in fact the images *are* accurate, then the future explosion *must* happen, despite Flint's best efforts to prevent it. The future is predetermined, and nothing can prevent the explosion from happening. Flint's actions may actually bring about the explosion, if the images are truly accurate. So the paradox is solved by getting rid of the conflict between Flint's freedom to prevent the future explosion and the accuracy of the images, by denying the first statement—namely, that Flint has the freedom to prevent the explosion. One might argue that it only looks as if she is free to prevent the event, but her supposed freedom is an illusion. Thus the subjective probability of the part of the paradox that claims that Flint can prevent the explosion is lowered.

One interesting result of treating paradoxes the way we are presently doing (i.e., using subjective probability) is that the very nature of paradox can be shown to be paradoxical. The following argument, modeled on the sorites paradox, is a paradox about paradoxes themselves—that is, a higher-order paradox:

Box 6

The paradoxicality paradox

1. An argument with a paradoxicality rating of 0 is nonparadoxical.
2. For any number n, if an argument with a paradoxicality rating of n is nonparadoxical, then an argument with a paradoxicality rating of (n + 0.001) is nonparadoxical.
3. An argument with a paradoxicality rating of 1 is nonparadoxical.

The paradoxicality of the previous argument is quite high. As in the sorites, both premises seem true; the argument's reasoning is straightforward; and the conclusion is, according to the definition of *paradoxicality*, conceptually false. Such an argument shows that the very concept of paradox is not immune from paradoxicality. Because paradoxes themselves admit of degrees, they too engender paradoxes. And because there are myriad paradoxes about a wide array of concepts, it makes sense that the concept of the paradox is itself paradoxical.

1.5 Conclusions

Taking intuition as the basis for paradoxes, and then analyzing our intuitions using subjective probability, we were
able to create the paradoxicality rating, which in turn gave
us a way of explaining why one paradox is deeper than another. We also have a way of making clearer the intuitions
that are necessary in order for something to be a paradox.
Solutions to paradoxes, we also saw, can be thought of as
pointing to a part of the paradox and then showing that
the subjective probability of the paradox should be lowered. Now that you have a fairly thorough understanding
of the intuitive basis of paradoxes, we can turn to the various solutions offered for them.

HOW TO SOLVE PARADOXES

2.1   Introduction: Solutions as Reeducations of Intuition

Imagine that you are a contestant on a game show. The host shows you three closed doors and tells you that there is a prize of a brand new car behind one door and goats behind each of the other two doors. You are then asked to choose a door. Once you make your selection of, say, Door #1, the host—who knows where the prize is hidden, and as he does with every contestant—opens another door, Door #3, to reveal a goat. He then gives you the option of switching your choice from Door #1 to Door #2.

   Should you switch? Is there any benefit from doing so? When asked this question, most people say that you are just as likely to win when you keep your first choice, Door #1, as if you switched your choice to Door #2. Most people say that when you made your first choice, you had a 1 in

3 chance of winning the car, and that now you have a 1 in 2 chance regardless of whether you go with Door #1 or Door #2, so switching doesn't matter. Actually, it turns out that our ordinary intuitions about switching turn out to be false. You would in fact increase your odds substantially by switching doors.

To see how this is so, imagine that you are now the game show host and know where the car is. If the contestant picks the correct door on the first try, then you can reveal either of the two other doors to the contestant and then make the offer to switch. But, what is the chance that this will happen? It is only 1 in 3, because initially the contestant has a one in three chance of getting the right door. So, it is two-thirds more likely that the contestant picked the wrong door. And if this is the case, then the car is behind one of the two remaining doors, and you, the host who knows where the car is, *must* open the only door with goat behind it. So, it is more likely that you had to open that door because it was the only door with the goat behind it that you could open. Because of this, the contestant has a much better shot of winning the car by switching than by staying with the original door.

This thought experiment, sometimes called the Monty Hall paradox (figure 2) after a famous game show host, nicely illustrates how some of the weaker paradoxes are solved (Clark 2007). Like the paradox of enrichment discussed in the introduction, this paradox confronts an

Figure 2 The Monty Hall paradox
Image taken from *Zen and the Art of Programming*, http://program
mingzen.com/2009/01/01/monte-carlo-simulation-of-the-monty-hall
-problem-in-ruby-and-python/.

intuition we have—in this case, about probability—and shows that our intuition is misleading. By showing that what we expected to be the case turns out to not be the case, we have "reeducated" our intuitions about probability. In the Monty Hall paradox, we did this by looking at the game show host's choices in the situation and showing that he is more likely to have revealed the only door with the goat behind it, leaving the remaining door the more likely winner and switching the better choice. This reeducation of intuition by showing that a counterintuitive consequence turns out to be true—that making the switch increases the contestant's chances—is a standard way of solving paradoxes.

Another way to reeducate our intuition about a part of the paradox is to show that the very notion that leads to the paradox is contradictory. An example of this can be seen by examining a standard solution to the barber paradox. Imagine that there is a remote town in the mountains of Sicily that has one barber, and that it is his job to shave all of the men in the town who don't shave themselves, and only those men. Does the barber then shave himself? If he does shave himself, then he doesn't, because he is not supposed to shave those who shave themselves. And if he doesn't shave himself, then he does, because his job is to shave those that do not shave themselves. One common way of dealing with the paradox is to say that there can be no such barber. Our intuitions that there could be such a barber are changed, upon further reflection, and we begin to lower the degree to which we believe one part of the paradox.

By reeducating our intuitions about the barber and our chances on the game show, we find a way out of the paradoxes. Earlier, you learned that a useful way to think about intuitions or "what we would say" in a given situation is using degrees of belief and is sometimes called *subjective probability*. You learned that when one of our beliefs had a high subjective probability—that is, close to 1—our rational beliefs were stronger. When our belief has a low subjective probability, such as 0.2, we are not believing at all, but disbelieving. And when the subjective probability of our belief is at 0.5, the midway point between complete disbelief (0) and complete certainty (1), we neither believe nor disbelieve. To solve paradoxes, then, usually means taking our intuitions about things such as chance, barbers who shave all and only the men who don't shave themselves, and so on and showing that the degrees to which we should rationally believe that our intuitions are correct should be lowered. Because subjective probability involves what a rational thinker believes, solutions attempt to provide rational grounds for lowering one's degrees of belief about the parts of the paradox. This "reeducation" of our intuitions, in which we send our intuitions back to school, as it were, can be done in numerous ways.

Table 3 Taxonomy of solution-types (strategies for solving paradoxes)

Solution-type	Explanation	Examples
Preemptive Strike: denying paradoxical notion	Claims that the paradox is of no concern because a central notion in it is fundamentally flawed, despite our immediate intuitions about it.	Sainsbury's account of the barber paradox
Odd-Guy-Out: identifying flawed statement in paradox	Claims that one supposedly plausible part of the paradox turns out to be false.	Timothy Williamson's solution to the sorites paradox
It's-All-Good: denying apparent inconsistencies	Claims that what looks like a set of mutually inconsistent statements can actually all be true at the same time. Or, if thinking of the paradox as an argument, claims that the conclusion is true.	Modern probability theory's solution to the Monty Hall paradox
You-Can't-Get-There-from-Here: showing reasoning in paradox is flawed	Shows that reasoning involved in generating the paradox is flawed.	Degree-theoretic solution to sorites paradox

Solution-type	Explanation	Examples
Detour: accepting the paradox, but providing alternative notion	Holds that the paradox exposes some basic conceptual flaw in the notion that leads to the paradox but provides an alternative interpretation of that notion that doesn't lead to paradox.	Tarski's solution to the liar paradox
Facing-the-Music: accepting the paradox, without providing alternative notion	Holds that the paradox exposes some basic conceptual flaw in notion that leads to paradox and that no acceptable replacement notion can be given.	Zeno's "solution" to his own "paradox"

Table 3 catalogs different strategies for solving para-doxes. I use the term *solution-type*, by which I mean a *strategy for analyzing paradoxes*. Two theories may give different solutions to the same or even different paradoxes, yet these two solutions may involve using the same strategy for analyzing the paradox and hence be part of the same solution-type. For example, as you'll see later, both Zeno of Elea and Michael Dummett use a Facing-the-Music solution to a paradox. Zeno held that no solution could be given to the paradoxes of space and motion he produced and Michael Dummett held that the sorites paradox admits of no plausible solution. Though they are concerned with different paradoxes, they both use the same general strategy for solving a paradox. They both say that the paradox can't be solved.

Let's examine each of these strategies for solving paradoxes in more detail. You may suspect, along the way, that this taxonomy, or catalog, of solution-types has an element of artificiality. If so, you are correct. Some solutions occupy border regions between types. And just as some paradoxes—such as Flint's paradox—can be characterized as a paradox about the nature of time, and also a paradox concerned with freedom of the will, solutions might not fit neatly into one solution-type, either.

Although detailed analyses of all the logical systems available for solving paradoxes is too big a task for any one book, it is helpful to look at some of the more promising systems and how they provide solutions to some of the more troubling paradoxes. The list includes systems from a variety of fields, including Zermelo-Fraenkel set theory, Bayesianism, degree-theoretic and fuzzy approaches, decision theory, and paraconsistent logic, among others. These systems are interesting in their own right and have important applications for present-day science, mathematics, and public policy. Bayesianism, for example, has influenced the way that scientists think about the evidence they collect. Zermelo-Fraenkel set theory embodies the best ways we have of thinking about collections of things. Fuzzy logic has uses in a wide range of areas: for example, the way patterns such as signatures are recognized by computers. And decision theory has important consequences for actions taken by governments, researchers, and others.

2.2 Solution-Type 1: The Preemptive Strike, or Questioning the Paradoxical Entity

Mark Sainsbury summarizes a popular solution to the barber paradox (concerning the barber in the remote town in Sicily who shaves all and only those men who do not shave themselves) in this way:

> The unacceptable supposition is that there is such a barber—one who shaves himself if, and only if, he does not. The story may have sounded acceptable; it turned our minds, agreeably enough, to the mountains of inland Sicily. However, once we see what the consequences are, we realize that the story cannot be true: There cannot be such a barber or such a village. The story is unacceptable. This is not a very deep paradox because the unacceptability is very thinly disguised by the mountains and the remoteness. (2009, 2)

To Sainsbury, our intuitions about the barber are wrong because we are lulled into believing that there can be things like barbers who shave all and only the men of the town who do not shave themselves. The paradoxicality rating of the barber would turn out to be fairly low, for the simple reason that the assumption that there can be such a barber is easily shown to be problematic.

Also, consider detective Flint and her dilemma of preventing a future explosion from happening. She was given images that, it was assumed, were accurate images of the future. But if she prevents the future explosion, how could the pictures have been accurate? One way to deal with this paradoxical situation is to deny that there can be accurate pictures of the future. One might argue that the images show what is likely going to happen, but not what will happen. Denying that there can be completely accurate predictions of the future allows for her to be able to prevent the explosion and even allows for some predictive power in the images.

A variety of this type of solution applies to paradoxes dealing with abstract concepts like statements and sets, and argues that the proposed abstract entity is either meaningless or self-contradictory. The simple liar sentence *This sentence is false* has been rejected, for example, on the grounds that it is meaningless and hence neither true nor false. In rejecting this sentence as somehow defective, this strategy preempts the basic liar paradox from arising in the first place.

To see how a logical system provides a preemptive strike against a paradox, let's take a look at Zermelo-Fraenkel set theory, and its treatment of Russell's paradox.

2.2.1 Example of a Preemptive Strike against a Paradox: Zermelo-Fraenkel Set Theory's Solution to Russell's Paradox

In 1902, after famed German logician Gottlob Frege received a letter from Bertrand Russell laying out what is now known as *Russell's paradox*, Frege responded to Russell as follows:

> Your discovery of the contradiction has caused me the greatest surprise and I would almost say, consternation, since it has shaken the basis on which I intended to build arithmetic. It seems. . . . that my Rule V is false. . . . I must reflect further on the matter. It is all the more serious since, with the loss of my Rule V, not only the foundation of my arithmetic, but also the sole possible foundations of arithmetic, seem to vanish. . . . In any case your discovery is remarkable, and will perhaps result in a great advance in logic, unwelcome as it may seem at first. (van Heijenoort 1967, 127–128)

The "Rule V" that Frege mentioned in his response to Russell was a basic principle of traditional "naive" set theory, a theory of sets that defines *set* informally. The principle is known as the *unrestricted comprehension principle*. According to this theory, every property has a set of things that satisfy that property, even if that set is the empty set. For example, being red is a property, so there is a set that corresponds to this property—namely, the set of red things. Under this early and basic way of thinking about what a set is, as long as something is a property—in other words, refers to a potential feature of reality such as being red, being a number, being prime, being a dog, and so on—there is a set that corresponds to it. And this condition is true even if nothing in actuality corresponds to this property. Even though no person instantiates the property of being the present king of New York (although Donald Trump might disagree), there is a set that corresponds to this property. It is the empty set. As long as there is a property, there is a set that corresponds to it. This statement is the *unrestricted comprehension axiom*, and Frege's Rule V.

The contradiction that prompted Frege's response to Russell was the paradoxical set R. With the paradoxical set R, the set that corresponds to the property of being "a set of all sets that do not contain themselves as members," a problem arises. If R is a member of itself, then it would be a member of the set that doesn't contain itself as a member, so then it wouldn't be a member of itself. And if R isn't a member of itself, then it would possess the property needed to be included in the set. So, it *would* be a member of itself:

Box 7

Russell's paradoxical set R

R: set of all sets that do not contain themselves
as members

Why not say here that something is defective about R?
That would be good, but the problem with this straightforward preemptive strike against the paradox is that there is
nothing, in principle, wrong with sets that contain other
sets as members. The set of sets with two members is an
example of this: {{1,2}, {a, b}, {0, 11}, {2, 5}, . . .}. Also, it
seems that some sets would contain themselves as members, such as the set of all sets, and that other sets wouldn't.
The set of all cups is not a cup, and hence wouldn't contain
itself as a member. But the set of all sets does possess the
property of being a set, so it would contain itself. The set
R is made up of sets themselves, too—specifically, the sets
that don't contain themselves as members. A member of
this set is the set of cups. The set of cups is not a cup, but
rather a set, so it counts as a set that does not contain itself
as a member. The set of roses is not a rose, and hence is
in the set of sets that don't contain themselves as members. So although saying that R is defective might be a good
strategy to take, the challenge is to say what it is about R,

and the naïve set theory that allows for it, that is not right. As this list progresses, the level of abstraction rises. We start with the most basic form of set, a set of objects—in this case, four cups. We then move to sets of numbers, then sets of sets, and finally to sets of sets with certain properties. Russell's set R is the seventh set in the following:

Box 8

Sample list of sets

1. A set of four cups {Cup 1, Cup 2, Cup 3, Cup 4}
2. The set of natural numbers, i.e., {1, 2, 3, . . .}
3. The set of natural numbers greater than 3, i.e., {4, 5, 6, . . .}
4. The set of sets that contain two members, i.e., {{a, b}, {1,2}, {101, 102}, . . .}
5. The set of all sets, i.e., {{a, b, c}, {0,1, 2, 3, . . .}, {Cup 1, Cup 2, Cup 3, Cup 4}, . . .}
6. The set of sets that contain themselves as members, i.e., {the set of all sets with more than 1 member, the set of all sets with more than 2 members, . . .}
7. The set of sets that don't contain themselves as members, i.e., {the set of cups, the set of roses, the set of sets with less than two members, . . .}

Zermelo-Fraenkel set theory (ZF), which is still standard today,[1] provides a way out of Russell's paradox. The basic strategy is to get rid of the unrestricted comprehension axiom, which holds that for any property there is a set of all things that satisfy that property. By this way of determining what can count as a set, we change our basic intuitions about what sets are and how they can be formed. ZF assumes that for any set and any definable property, there is a subset of all the elements of the given set that satisfy that property. Under this approach, you don't start with a property and then say that there is a set that corresponds to it. Instead, you start with a set and property, and then say that for this set and property there is a subset of all the elements of the set that satisfy the property. What's the difference? You might think of it as the difference between a top down approach on naive set theory, and a bottom up approach on ZF. Instead of starting with a property and then finding the objects that satisfy that property, you start with individuals and make sets that satisfy any given property. According to ZF, R cannot be constructed. Nor can a set of all sets, for that matter, because you are using a bottom-up approach by constructing sets and saying what subsets of that given set satisfy a property.

Zermelo-Fraenkel set theory provides a "preemptive strike" against Russell's paradox in that it gives rules for the construction of sets that precludes the problematic "set of all sets that do not contain themselves as members." To see how it does this in greater detail, it is necessary to more fully understand the theory.

ZF is an axiomatic set theory. The theory starts with certain *axioms*, that is, primitive claims that are taken as assumptions without any further justification within the system. ZF also contains *primitive notions*, which are given definitions without further justification within the system. A primitive notion that is defined by ZF is that of a *well-founded set*. This set, for ZF, is a hereditary set—that is, one in which all members of the set are themselves sets, as well as all of their elements, and so on. In a hereditary set, the member sets go all the way down, as it were. ZF also contains a primitive relation, that of *set membership*, which is represented with the symbol ϵ. So, $a \epsilon b$ can be read as *a is a member of b* or *a is in b*. This symbol is used along with the other symbols of first-order logic in ZF.

The axioms of ZF, particularly the axiom schema[2] of restricted comprehension, give us an understanding of sets on which the set R turns out to be unacceptable and hence the paradox turns out to be averted. Let's look at some of these axioms. The first axiom, the axiom of extensionality, holds that any two sets are equal if they have the same members. The second axiom, the axiom of regularity, holds that every nonempty set A contains at least one element B that has no members in A. Another way to put this is to say that every set that is nonempty contains an element that is "disjoint" from the set. What's the point of saying this? It means that, for a nonempty set A, there must be a B that is an element of A, and A and B must be distinct to the point that every member of B is not in A. You might wonder how something that is a member of B—let's call it C—is not also a member of A, given that B is a member of A. Remember, though, that B is a set that is a member of A, so C is not, strictly speaking, also an member of A. One of the consequences of this axiom is that A cannot be a member of itself. For the purposes of Russell's paradox, this axiom is important. The axiom draws a strong distinction between sets and the things that they contain. It keeps a strict hierarchy between sets and their members, so that sets cannot be members at the same time.

The axiom schema of ZF also has important implications for Russell's paradox. The *axiom schema of restricted comprehension* asserts that given any set and any property that may (or may not) characterize the elements of that set, there is a subset of the set that contains all the elements that satisfy that property. For example, consider the set x, which is {red, 12, c, blue}, and the property of being a color. For this set, there is a subset, {red, blue}, that satisfies the property of being a color. There are other subsets of the set for other properties, such as being a natural number ({12}), or being a clown (the empty set). So the basic point of the axiom schema is that any definable subclass of a set is itself a set. For Russell's paradox, this point is important because under ZF a property doesn't determine a set.

Instead, *given a set* and *given a property*, some things will satisfy the property and others will not.

Because, according to this theory, R—the set of all sets that do not contain themselves as members cannot exist—the paradox dissolves. Yet by creating a system under which the R set is not well-founded, and hence avoiding the paradox, the ZF approach also has some troubling consequences. For example, there is no way to construct a set of all sets. But shouldn't there be such a set? Also, what about the set of all cardinal numbers (i.e., numbers that tell the size of sets)? This set cannot be constructed via Zermelo-Fraenkel set theory, either. More generally, the naive notion that any property determines a set more closely resembles, it seems, common intuitions about sets. The additional stipulation that a set of items, a subclass of which satisfies the property may seem to some to be an ad hoc way to avoid the paradox. So, like many solutions to paradoxes, the theory meant to resolve the paradox leads to some troubling consequences.

2.2.2 General Analysis of the Preemptive-Strike Solution-Type

The Preemptive-Strike method for solving paradoxes, by calling into question the very notion that leads to paradox, reduces the subjective probability that there can be such a notion. As a result, the subjective probabilities associated with the assumptions of the paradox are lowered as well.

This type of solution is successful only when the entity that gives rise to the paradox is easily forsaken or can be revised with little loss to the original notion. The world won't miss barbers who shave all and only those men who do not shave themselves, but sets are important to mathematics and even how we organize the world around us. If there is some fundamental flaw in our notion of what makes a set, then our use of sets—and perhaps even the way we think about all collections of entities—might be in error. Thus, if a solution such as the Zermelo-Fraenkel theory, in rejecting the paradoxical set R, cannot adequately preserve the fundamental notion of a set, then the solution must be considered inadequate.

The paradoxes that can be solved by denying the existence or meaningfulness or consistency of the entity that leads to the paradox, therefore, are usually fairly weak paradoxes. If the entity can be so easily dismissed in this way, the paradox wouldn't call into question our most deeply held and useful concepts.

2.3 Solution-Type 2: The Odd-Guy-Out Approach, or Pointing to the Flawed Assumption

One of the ways to define *paradox* is *an argument with seemingly true premises (assumptions), apparently good reasoning, and an obviously false, or contradictory conclusion.* Because good reasoning from true premises should lead to a true conclusion, paradoxes make us question the premises from which we derive our conclusions. Thus a very common way of solving a paradox is to point to one of these premises and show that it is in fact false. This method is embodied in many solutions to paradoxes, whether we think of paradoxes as sets of assumptions, arguments, faulty conclusions drawn from apparently correct premises, or any plausible definition of the term *paradox*. Following is an example.

2.3.1 The Unexpected Examination

One day in class, a teacher announces that an unexpected examination (see table 4) will occur on any day at noon during the following school week. In response to the teacher's announcement, a student decides that this cannot be. If the exam were held on Friday, then the exam would be expected to happen by Thursday afternoon, because all the other possible days have been eliminated. So Friday is ruled out. And if the exam were held Thursday then it would eventually be expected, too, because Friday has already been ruled out, leaving Thursday as the last possible day. But now the same goes for Wednesday and the other days of the week, including Monday. Monday is the last remaining option, but if the exam were to be held on Monday, given that all the other days were already eliminated, it would not be unexpected. Therefore, there can be no

Because good reason-
ing from true premises
should lead to a true
conclusion, paradoxes
make us question the
premises from which we
derive our conclusions.

Table 4 The unexpected examination

Possible day for exam	Reasons to exclude day from being the day of the unexpected examination
Friday	Would be last possible day to hold exam, and if the exam were held on Friday, it would not be a surprise.
Thursday	Given that Friday has been eliminated, Thursday is now the last possible day to hold the exam. But if the exam is now given on Thursday, it would not be unexpected, because Friday has been eliminated.
Wednesday	Given that Friday and Thursday have now been eliminated, Wednesday is now the last possible day to hold the exam. But if the exam were given on Wednesday, it would not be unexpected, because Friday and Thursday have already been eliminated.
Tuesday	Given that Friday, Thursday, and Wednesday now have been eliminated, Tuesday is the last possible day to hold the exam. But, if the exam were given on Tuesday, it wouldn't be unexpected, because Friday, Thursday and Wednesday have already been eliminated.
Monday	Monday is now the only day left on which to hold the exam. However, given that this is so, if the exam were to be held on Monday, it would not be unexpected.

unexpected exam. After reasoning along these lines, the student does not prepare for the exam, and lo and behold, an exam takes place on Wednesday of the following week at noon, much to the contrary of the student's expectation. But how could this be? What in the student's argument was wrong?

The teacher's announcement may itself seem paradoxical, given that the teacher is announcing that the exam will happen next week, although not announcing the particular day of the exam. In saying, "You will have an exam next week that is unexpected, and I'm announcing it now," at least some expectation is developing, and the exam won't be completely unexpected, unless you are the student who concludes that the exam cannot happen. One solution to this paradox, then, is that the student's argument assumes a specific interpretation of "unexpected exam," one on which the exam day must be not determined at any point before the time of the exam. This is a very strong interpretation of how unexpected the exam will be. Another way to interpret the teacher's announcement is that an exam will take place on a day that is not capable of being determined until the very last option is the only one available. In changing this assumption, the elimination of Friday as an option cannot happen, and neither can the subsequent elimination of Thursday, Wednesday, and so on. Thus, an assumption that must be made in order to motivate the paradox is called into question. Similarly, we might interpret the teacher's announcement that there will be an unexpected examination as saying that there is nothing based on the teacher's announcement that would allow the students to determine which is the day of the exam.

For a more thoroughgoing Odd-Guy-Out-type solution to a paradox, consider the Bayesian solution to the Quine/Duhem problem, which can be put in the form of a paradox. This solution is especially relevant to us because we have used a key Bayesian idea, that of subjective probability (degrees of belief), to analyze paradoxes. As explained in the following section, Bayesians use the idea of subjective probability, coupled with Bayes' theorem, in their attempt to solve a key problem regarding scientific confirmation.

2.3.2 Watchmakers, Doctors, Scientists: Bayesianism and the Quine/Duhem Paradox

Willard Quine and Pierre Duhem raised a problem for what is traditionally known as the *hypothetico-deductive model* of scientific hypothesis testing. According to this traditional model, a scientific hypothesis is tested by deducing an observable consequence of the hypothesis and then empirically observing whether this consequence actually is the case. That is, with H representing the hypothesis, $\rightarrow$ meaning that what follows is a consequence, and e standing for the evidence for the following hypothesis:

Box 9

The hypothetico-deductive model

1. H → *e*
2. Not *e*
3. Therefore, not H

Under this model of scientific testing, a logical consequence *e* is derived from the hypothesis *H*, and then *e* is observed. In the event that *e* turns out to be disconfirmed, then according to this model, the hypothesis *H* is shown to be false. The relevant rule of inference here is called *modus tollens*. Here's a rough example of the kind of reasoning involved. Assume that I am a scientist and my hypothesis *H* is that drinking coffee causes cancer. A logical consequence of my hypothesis is that when a group of people with similar health histories and habits are divided into the coffee drinkers and non–coffee drinkers, there will be a significantly higher occurrence of cancer among the coffee drinkers than the non–coffee drinkers. The *e* in this case is the claim that there will be a significantly greater occurrence of cancer in the coffee drinkers. Suppose I test the hypothesis and find no such significant difference. On the traditional hypothetico-deductive model of scientific testing, this evidence proves conclusively that the hypothesis that coffee causes cancer is false. If, though, a significant difference is shown, this does not conclusively prove the truth of the hypothesis. Suppose then I do the experiment and discover a significant difference. It shows only that the hypothesis has passed one test because, logically speaking, there could be some other factor that brings about the greater occurrence of cancer in the subjects that were the coffee drinkers, other than the drinking of coffee.

Pierre Duhem (1954, 185) made the following critique of this model of scientific testing: "The [scientist] can never submit an isolated hypothesis to the control of experiment, but only a whole group of hypotheses. When experiment is in disagreement with his predictions, it teaches him that one at least of the hypotheses that constitute this group is wrong and must be modified. But experiment does not show him the one that must be changed." For example, if, in testing my hypothesis about coffee and cancer, subjects weren't controlled for their eating of raw spinach, it might turn out that raw spinach eating in the non–coffee drinkers was what protected them from cancer, not their avoidance of coffee.

Duhem's problem is with the first part of the hypothetico-deductive model, $(H \rightarrow e)$. His claim is that no hypothesis can be separated from an indefinite set of auxiliary hypotheses. In our coffee example, an auxiliary premise might be that the test was done on a group of people with similar health histories, or that there was no mistake in the counting of the instances, and so on. Taking into consideration this indefinite set of auxiliary premises (A1, . . . , An), we then have the following:

Box 10

The Quine/Duhem problem

1. {H, (A1, A2, A3, . . . , An)} → e
2. Not e
3. Not {H, (A1, A2, A3, . . . , An)}

So *H* is supplemented with an indefinite set of *A*s, and if Duhem is right, then all the conflicting result shows is that one of the set of the main and auxiliary hypotheses is mistaken. What the result does not show any longer is *not H*. In our example, the lack of a significant difference is no longer conclusive grounds for rejecting the hypothesis that coffee causes cancer.

Duhem (1954, 187–188) sometimes explained his problem by comparing the scientist to a doctor and contrasting the scientist with a watchmaker. A watchmaker, when faced with a watch that does not work, can look at each part of the watch in isolation, going from piece to piece, until the defect is detected. The doctor, on the other hand, cannot examine each of the parts of an ailing patient's body in isolation. Instead, she must detect the seat of the illness only by inspecting the effects produced on the whole body. Similarly, the scientist cannot separate out each of an indefinite set of auxiliary premises to test each in isolation. From this, though, a paradox arises, one concerning how it is reasonable to "lay blame" on a main scientific hypothesis versus one of the hypothesis' auxiliaries:

Box 11

The simple Quine/Duhem paradox

1. No hypothesis can be tested in isolation from an indefinite set of auxiliary hypotheses.
2. In order to show that a hypothesis is mistaken, it is necessary to isolate that hypothesis from its set of auxiliary hypotheses.
3. Therefore, no hypothesis can be shown to be mistaken.

The first premise of the previous argument is the claim that whenever a test of a hypothesis is made, there is an indefinite set of auxiliary hypotheses that must go along with the hypothesis. For another example, imagine an experiment that is designed to test the hypothesis that the earth has the shape of a cube by observing the shadow it casts during an eclipse (figure 3).

The hypothesis is that the earth is a cube, and an entailment of this hypothesis is that the earth will leave a square or diamond-shaped shadow. But the earth's shadow is an entailment only if certain other preconditions are met. For example, the experimenter assumes the following: the light will not be such that it turns the shadows of cubes into circles, the instruments used to identify the shadow are functioning properly, and so on. The first premise implies that the cube hypothesis, in order to be tested, must accompany these and an indefinite set of other hypotheses. But a negative experimental result shows only that there is something wrong with the set of hypotheses (*H, A1, A2, . . . , An*) and not with *H* itself. It is this type of argument that licenses premise two of the simple Quine/ Duhem paradox—namely, the statement that there must be some way of isolating *H* from all the auxiliary premises, if one is going to be able to that it is mistaken.

The second premise of the simple Quine/Duhem paradox implies that for the cube hypothesis to be shown to be mistaken, the hypothesis must be separated from its auxiliary premises. Assume that the cube-shaped earth experiment is performed and the shadow is circular. In this case, the circular shadow shows only that one of the set of hypotheses that includes *H* and an indefinite set of auxiliary

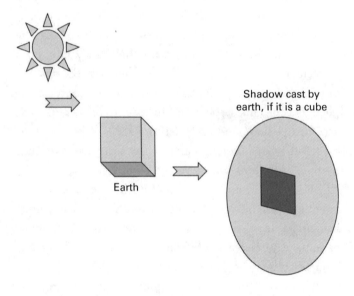

Shadow cast by
earth, if it is a cube

Earth

Figure 3 Sample hypothesis and entailment

hypotheses is mistaken. What it does not show is that *H* is mistaken. The conclusion of the simple form of the paradox is that no hypothesis can be shown to be mistaken. In the case of the cube hypothesis, this hypothesis cannot be shown to be mistaken, either.

The Quine/Duhem problem, phrased as a paradox, is really a special case of a skeptical paradox that claims that the incredibly strong precondition for my knowing *p* cannot be attained, and hence I cannot know *p*. For example, I can know that I am in New York right now only if I am certain that I'm not dreaming. But I can't be completely certain of my not being dreaming (I could have nodded off while writing, for example), so I can't know that I'm in New York right now. For the Quine/Duhem paradox, the set of auxiliary premises has the same function as the precondition in the skeptical paradox: because they cannot be ruled out, they keep us from knowing the status of the hypothesis. The conclusion of the skeptical paradox is that we cannot know some obvious hypothesis (we can't prove *H*), while for the Quine/Duhem paradox the conclusion is that no hypothesis can be shown to be mistaken (we can't prove *not H*).

A group of philosophers of statistics claim to have a solution to the Quine/Duhem problem. These philosophers, known as *Bayesians*, get their name from the statistician Thomas Bayes. According to the Bayesians, an answer to the Quine/Duhem problem can be given if the hypothetico-deductive model of scientific testing is replaced with another model. According to the Bayesian model, evidence *e* confirms a hypothesis *H* to the extent that a scientist's degree of belief in *H* is higher given evidence *e* than what it was or would be without this evidence. As discussed in chapter 1, subjective probability is a measure of the subjective degree of belief ranging from 0 or complete disbelief to 1 or complete certainty. The scientist's degree of belief in the hypothesis without the evidence is called the *prior probability* of the hypothesis, and the scientist's degree of belief in the hypothesis after the evidence is called the *posterior probability*. So if the posterior probability of *H* is greater than the prior probability of *H*, the extent to which *H* is confirmed is the difference between the posterior and prior probabilities. To figure out the posterior probability of *H*, Bayesians use a version of Bayes' theorem:

Box 12

Bayes' theorem

$$P(H \mid e) = \frac{P(e \mid H)\, P(H)}{P(e \mid H)\, P(H) + P(e \mid \text{not-}H)\, P(\text{not-}H)}$$

This statement is read as "The probability of *H*, given *e*, is equal to the probability of *e* given *H* multiplied by the probability of *H*, over the probability of *e* given *H*, times the probability of *H*, plus the probability of *e* given *not-H* times the probability of *not-H*." It means that the probability of a scientific hypothesis given a new piece of evidence is determined in the following way: take the probability of the evidence happening given that the hypothesis is true (for example, the probability that the Earth would cast a square shadow, given that it is a cube), then multiply this by the probability of the hypothesis alone (e.g., the probability that the Earth is a cube all by itself). Then, divide this number by itself plus the probability of the evidence happening if the hypothesis is not the case (e.g., the square shadow with an Earth that isn't a cube), times the probability that the hypothesis is not the case (e.g., the probability that Earth is not a cube).

Certain factors need to be known before this calculation and the "laying of blame" can take place: (1) the prior probabilities in *H* and *not-H*; (2) the likelihood, which is *P(e | H)*; and (3) what's called the Bayesian "catchall factor," which is *P (e | not-H)*, which is the probability of the evidence, without the hypothesis being the case. Once you have these, then you just plug them into Bayes' theorem to get the posterior probability, which tells how well the evidence confirms the hypothesis.

Here's an example: consider a situation in which an experiment is done and the result seems to contradict the hypothesis in question. One response to this negative result would be to reject the hypothesis. Think back to the coffee example. Another response would be to look at the auxiliary premises. Suppose for simplicity's sake that there is only one auxiliary premise, that the subjects in the study have similar health histories. In this case, the main hypothesis H is that coffee causes cancer, and the auxiliary hypothesis A is that a test of the hypothesis will involve people who have similar health histories. In this simplified example, hypothesis H and auxiliary A entail e, a significant difference in cancer occurrence, but *not-e* is observed. The Bayesian account shows when A is more likely to be blamed than H, or vice versa. Assume that there is a great deal of evidence for H and that there is hardly more evidence for the truth of A than there is evidence for A's falsity. In our example, perhaps the health histories of the subjects weren't checked very thoroughly, so it is possible that the coffee drinkers also smoke and the non–coffee drinkers don't. In this situation, it is more likely that A is where the problem lies, rather than H. Bayesians solve this type of problem by plugging in values into Bayes' theorem. First, they assign a lower prior probability to A than to H. For example, A, being only slightly more probable than *not* A, it would have a prior probability of around 0.6. H, on the other hand, would have a very high probability, say 0.9. Second, with regard to the likelihood, the Bayesians assign a far greater likelihood for the negative result to happen when *not-A* is true rather than *not H*. For example, P(not-e | a) = x, and P(not-e | not-a and H) = 50x, and P(not-e |

not-a and not-H) = 50x. I'll spare you the calculations.[3] The result is that after plugging these numbers into Bayes' theorem, the probability of H is only slightly decreased, going from 0.9 to 0.897, whereas the probability of A plummets from 0.6 to 0.003. So, given their prior probabilities, and the likelihood of getting the *not-e* result when either A or H is not true, it follows that the scientist has good reason to reject A, while still preserving H.

In a nutshell, the Bayesians, by analyzing the subjective degrees of belief of the scientists and plugging these probabilities into Bayes' theorem, attempt to give an account of when the rejection of the main hypothesis is warranted and when an auxiliary premise is instead what must be rejected. The Bayesians solve the Quine/Duhem paradox by rejecting the second premise, the one which claims that in order to show that a hypothesis is mistaken, it is necessary to isolate that hypothesis from its set of auxiliary hypotheses. As long as we know the prior beliefs in the auxiliary premises, we can determine whether they should be rejected.

Although this is the standard view of scientific reasoning about Duhemian problems in the philosophy of statistics, the Bayesian account has certain problems. The most important objection concerns the Bayesians' reliance on the prior degree of belief of the scientist in his or her hypothesis before the hypothesis is tested. Assuming that scientists have such degrees of belief, and also assuming that these beliefs can be quantified into degrees, it is undesirable that the prior beliefs be taken as central to reasoning in science. Such subjective beliefs are highly variable, changing not only from person to person, but also in the same person from moment to moment. There are some beliefs to which all rational believers would assign 0, such as an obvious contradiction. However, most beliefs don't work this way. For example, if a scientist's belief varies even slightly during a day, the justification for the acceptance or rejection of a hypothesis will be altered. Something seems not right with this subjectivist account. The problem, I suspect, lies in the conflation of a scientist's confidence in his or her hypothesis with the evidence that it is true. As Deborah Mayo asks in the title of an article critiquing the Bayesian approach, "What's Belief Got to Do with It?":

> Scientists do not succeed in justifying a claim that an anomaly is due not to H but to an auxiliary hypothesis by describing the degrees of belief that would allow them to do this. On the contrary, scientists are one in blocking an attempted explanation of an anomaly until and unless it is provided with positive evidence in its own right. And what they would need to show is that this evidence succeeds in circumventing the many ways of erroneously attributing blame. (1997, 228–229)

Here Mayo is critiquing the white-glove treatment given by the Bayesians as to how to solve such problems. To determine when an anomalous result requires that the main hypothesis or some auxiliary hypothesis to be rejected requires more than the subjective degrees of belief of the scientist prior to the experiment. What is required is evidence that the auxiliary is the faulty assumption and an account of why this evidence isn't mistakenly taken as evidence that the auxiliary is to blame.

The use of subjective probability in the Bayesian account of the Quine/Duhem paradox, to my mind, is less warranted than using subjective probability for looking at paradoxes, for the simple reason that paradoxes are inherently about our beliefs and the ways in which strong beliefs conflict.

2.3.3 Zeno's Paradoxes and the Idea of an Infinitely Converging Series

Another example of the Odd-Guy-Out solution comes from modern mathematics' conception of a *convergent geometric series*, which provides a standard way of solving many of Zeno's paradoxes. Many of Zeno's paradoxes, which will be discussed in detail later in this book, call into question ordinary ideas about space, time, and motion. In the paradox of the dichotomy, for example, Zeno argues that a person cannot travel from any point A to any point B, because to get from A to B, the person would have to get to the halfway point, and to get to the halfway point, the person would have to get to the halfway point between A and the halfway point, and to get to this point the person would have to go halfway between A and this point, and so on, ad infinitum. And because a person cannot make an infinite amount of journeys in a finite time, the person cannot get from point A to point B.

To help solve the paradox, modern mathematics uses the notion of an infinitely converging geometric series. A *geometric series* is a series with a constant ratio between successive terms. For example, in the series 16, 8, 4, 2, . . . the next number can be obtained by multiplying the previous number by ½. The multiplication of each number by ½ to result in the next means that the series has a constant ratio of ½. Notice that we have indicated that the series is infinite by using an ellipsis. But is the sum of this series finite? You might think that because there is an infinite number of items in the series that if you add all the items together, the sum of the items would be infinite, too. But such does not turn out to be the case.

Consider the series ½, ¼, ⅛, . . . The sum of this series will not be an infinite number, but 1. To see how this is so, it is helpful to introduce the concept of a *convergent series*. A *convergent series* has a constant ratio of less than 1 but greater than –1. In this case, the items in the series get closer and closer toward the limit of 0. The series ½, ¼,

⅛, . . . has a common ratio of ½, which means that it is a convergent series. The next number in the series is ¹⁄₁₆, followed by ¹⁄₃₂, and so on. Notice how the fractions get smaller and smaller. But will they ever reach 0 in this series? No. The numbers will continue to be reduced by half, but half of any number that is greater than 0 will be greater than 0. Because it is a convergent series, its sum is finite, not infinite. To figure out the sum of an infinite convergent series, we divide the common ratio into the series. So let's call the series s. For example, s = ½, ¼, ⅛, . . . The common ratio of this series is ½. Multiplying into the series, we then have ½s = ¼, ⅛, ¹⁄₁₆, . . . In this series, the only difference is that the first item in the series (½) is missing. So, when we subtract the new series from the old one, we get the exact same series minus the first item. So, s − ½s = ½, and if we solve for s, we get s = 1. Thus the sum of the series that is used in Zeno's paradox of the dichotomy is equal to 1. Yet one assumption made by the paradox was that it is impossible for a distance to be divided infinitely, without that distance itself being infinite. According to this solution, it is indeed possible for this to happen. Hence, Zeno's paradox is given an Odd-Guy-Out solution using the notion of the infinite convergent series. The premise that states that one cannot travel across an infinitely divisible space, because one would then have to make an infinite amount of small "journeys" is false.

2.3.4 General Analysis of the Odd-Guy-Out Solution-Type

What the previously discussed solutions to the unexpected examination, Quine/Duhem, and Zeno's paradoxes have in common is that each points to an assumption made by the relevant part of the paradox and attempts to call that assumption into question. Each solution provides reason for lowering the subjective probability of that part of the paradox. In the case of the unexpected examination, the solution makes us rethink what "unexpected examination" entails and conclude that the teacher could not have meant that the examination could not have been expected on Friday. Given an alternative assumption that the teacher meant that the exam day could not be expected until after Thursday's exam period was over, the paradox is made easier to treat. Similarly, the Bayesian account of scientific confirmation provides a way of showing that one assumption made by the Quine/Duhem paradox—namely, that no hypothesis can be tested in isolation from the others—was mistaken. And the solution to Zeno's dichotomy involved confronting our intuitive thought that infinite series cannot have a finite sum. All three of these solutions attempt to get us to reject an assumption made by the paradox. Another way to think of this approach is in terms of subjective probability. Where we once believed in the truth of the assumption, our degree of belief in this assumption is now lowered dramatically.

As a general strategy for paradox solution, the Odd-Guy-Out approach is successful to the degree that it is capable of lowering the subjective probability of an assumption in the paradox. As we can see with Bayesian solution to the Quine/Duhem paradox, lowering our subjective probability about one assumption often entails further assumptions that are themselves implausible. Thus, to lower the subjective probability of one part of the paradox, these solutions often introduced further assumptions with even lower subjective probabilities. Even the solution to the Zeno's paradox involves a revision of our ordinary folk ideas about space and infinite divisibility. The success of an Odd-Guy-Out approach is often undercut by its introduction of yet another assumption with a low subjective probability.

2.4 Solution-Type 3: You-Can't-Get-There-from-Here, or Denying the Validity of the Reasoning

The You-Can't-Get-There-from-Here solution-type claims that although the assumptions made by the paradox are fine, these assumptions do not lead to the conclusion. Whereas the Odd-Guy-Out solution-type points to a flawed assumption, You-Can't-Get-There-from-Here says that the assumptions are not the problem, but rather that the problem lies in thinking that they lead to an obviously false conclusion. Such a strategy takes issue with the underlying reasoning of the paradox. An example of this type of strategy comes from the contextualist solution to a skeptical paradox:

Box 13

A skeptical paradox

1. I can know for sure that I am in New York only if I can know that I am not dreaming.
2. I cannot know that I am not dreaming.
3. Therefore, I cannot know for sure that I am in New York.

A contextualist solution to this paradoxical argument involves pointing to an equivocation in the meaning of the crucial term *know* (Schiffer 1996). Standards for "knowability" vary in different contexts, claims the contextualist. To know that one is in New York in the ordinary sense involves far less stringent criteria than the knowledge that hinges on certainty. Thus, *know* in the first premise of the argument means something different than *knows* in the second premise. The argument is therefore invalid, according to the contextualist. Although it initially looks as if it takes the valid argument form given earlier, the actual argument form of the skeptical paradox is the invalid form, in which an additional term has to be introduced because P refers to one specific form of knowledge, a garden-variety knowledge with low need for proof, and R refers to another type of knowledge—namely, knowledge that I am not radically deceived, which requires a good deal of proof. Because an argument of this form is invalid, claims the contextualist, the paradox dissolves:

Box 14

Invalid argument form

1. P, only if Q
2. Not R
3. Therefore, not P

2.4.1 A Systematic You-Can't-Get-There-from-Here Solution: Fuzzy Logic's Solution to the Sorites Paradox

Fuzzy logic, like many-valued logics, adds additional values to traditional two-valued logic and semantics. According to classical logic and semantics, a concept is a function from objects to the set {0,1}, where "0" represents falsity and "1" represents truth. So, for each object, a concept maps the object either to truth or to falsity. In the case of the concept "round," for example, the concept maps a basketball to truth and most computers to falsity. On the fuzzy account, however, a concept is a function from objects that takes values in the unit interval [0,1], where "0" stands for falsity and "1" stands for truth. On the fuzzy account, an object may be 0.7-round, instead of completely round or completely not-round (e.g., a long watermelon might fall in between complete roundness and complete nonroundness).

Kenton Machina (1976), who uses Jan Lukasiewickz's system Lx, claims that the truth conditions for degrees of truth will obey table 5: the first rule states that the truth-value of a statement's denial is determined by subtracting that value from 1. For example, if a statement is 0.70-true, then its denial is 0.30-true. An utterance of *This glass is full* is 0.50-true when the glass is filled halfway; an utterance of *This glass is empty* is 0.50-true if the glass is filled halfway as well.

Table 5   Fuzzy truth-conditions

Let /P/ mean *the value of P*.

1. $/-P/ = 1 - /P/$

2. $/P \ \& \ Q/ = \text{Min}(/P/, /Q/)$

3. $/P \lor Q/ = \text{Max}(/P/, /Q/)$

4. $/P \rightarrow Q/ = 1$ where $/Q/ > /P/$; or $= 1 - /P/ + /Q/$ where $/P/ > /Q/$

5. $/(\forall x)A(x)/$ = the greatest lower bound of the values $/A(t)/$ for each name t

6. $/(\exists x)A(x)/$ = the least upper bound of the values $/A(t)/$ for each name t

The second rule states that the truth-value of a conjunction is determined by taking the minimum value of the two conjuncts. Consider the conjunction (A & B), where A is 0.55-true and B is 0.65-true. The conjunction is 0.55-true, because this is the lesser truth-value of the two.[4] The third rule states that the truth-value of a disjunction is determined by taking the maximum value of its two disjunctions. Consider the disjunction (A v B), that is, (A OR B), where A is 0.55-true and B is 0.65-true. The truth-value for this disjunction is 0.65, because this is the greater of the two numbers. It makes sense that the combined truth-value of the conjuncts (parts of an *AND* statement) would be the lower of the two conjuncts, because there is a more stringent requirement on conjunctions—namely, that both be true. Equally, it makes sense that the truth-value of a disjunction (*OR* statement) should be the higher value of the two disjuncts.

The truth-conditions for conditionals (*If P, then Q* statements) are important for the present discussion, because the inductive premise (IP) is a conditional statement. According to the fourth rule, a conditional is completely true (i.e., has a truth-value of 1) if the consequent (Q) has a greater degree of truth than the antecedent (P). If, on the other hand, the antecedent has a greater value than the consequent, then the truth-value of the conditional is determined by subtracting the antecedent's value from 1 and adding the result to the consequent's value. Thus, when the antecedent has a greater value than the consequent, a conditional is true to the degree that its antecedent is false *and* its consequent true. For example, if P has a truth-value of 0.60 and Q a value of 0.20, then the truth-value of (P → Q) is (1 – 0.60) + 0.20, or 0.60.

Whereas in classical logic, a conditional (P → Q) translates into the disjunction of the negation of its antecedent and the assertion of its consequent (~P v Q), in fuzzy logic, this translation cannot be made. To see why conditionals do not translate into disjunctions in fuzzy logic, consider a conditional (P → P) for which P's value is ½. If we could translate conditionals into disjunctions, the truth-value of this conditional would be (~P v P), which is the maximum value of the two disjuncts, which is ½. But this conditional, it seems, must be completely true, because P *must* entail P, because P necessarily has the same truth-value as itself. According to this type of fuzzy logic, though, the conditional (P → P) has the truth-value 1 – /P/ + /P/, which is (1 – ½) + ½, or 1. So, by this account, this conditional is completely true.

As for the last two fuzzy truth conditions, (5) holds that for a generalization, such as *All men are mortal*, the truth value is determined by the lower bound of the set of sentences that take the form *A is a man and A is mortal*. The lower bound is the value that is lower or equal to every member of the set. The upper bound is the value that is greater or equal to each member of the set. So (6) holds that for claims such as *There is a man that is mortal*, the value of this statement is the value highest or equal to every member of the set of sentences that take the form *A is a man and A is mortal*. Put simply, for (5), because generalizations (*All s are P*) are true to the degree that every *s* is P, the lowest value for any *s is P* statement is the one that stands for the whole generalization. It makes sense, because to refute a claim such as *All men are mortal*, you would point to a counterinstance, that is, a man who is not mortal. The truth of the generalization is thus lowered by the value of a counterinstance. And, for (6), because all you need to prove that *There exists a man and he is mortal* is to prove that there is one such man, you take the highest value of statements of the form *A is a man and A is mortal*.

On the fuzzy account, the sorites paradox starts with a completely true statement as its first premise—for example, *A man with 0 hairs on his head is bald*. Then, via a series of premises of the form *If a man with n hairs on his head is bald, then a man with (n + 1) hairs on his head is bald*, a completely false conclusion is drawn. The middle premises in this long series have antecedents (*A man with* n *hairs on his head is bald*) that are just a little more true than their consequents (*A man with (n + 1) hairs on his head is bald*). For example, consider the following:

Box 15

A step in the sorites paradox

1. A man with 0 hairs on his head is bald.
2. If a man with 0 hairs on his head is bald, then a man with (0 + 1) hairs on his head is bald.
3. A man with 1 hair on his head is bald.

The conclusion of this argument can then be the first premise of another argument, using the same form of the middle premise, *If a man with 1 hairs on his head is bald, then a man with (1+1) hairs on his head is bald*, leading to the conclusion *A man with 2 hairs on his head is bald*. And so on, until the conclusion *A man with 100,000 hairs is bald* is reached.

Because a man with no hair is balder than a man with one hair, the antecedent of the premises that take the form *If a man with n hairs on his head is bald, then a man with (n + 1) hairs on his head is bald* is truer than the consequent. One might then conclude that premises taking this form are completely false because their consequents are not as true as their antecedents, and because the consequent of a true conditional should be at least as true as its antecedent.

However, the fuzzy logician is not so much concerned with the preservation of perfect truth as with the preservation of degrees of truth. On classical logic, the only way for an "if-then" ($P \rightarrow Q$) statement to be false is for the antecedent (P) to be true and the consequent (Q) false. According to fuzzy logic, this definition is altered to account for degrees of truth. In the case of premise 2 as discussed earlier, the antecedent is completely true (1). The truth-value of the consequent is almost completely true, so that second premise will have a truth-value of the denial of the antecedent (0) + the value of the consequent, which is almost 1. As the number n increases, the antecedent becomes less true, and hence its denial more true; also, the consequent becomes less true.

The conclusion of the previous argument is not as true as the first premise. And as further arguments are constructed with the conclusion of one argument being the first premise of the next, then the conclusions of these new arguments would be progressively less true than their first premises and even less true than the first premise of the first argument. After a series of such arguments, the conclusions will be almost perfectly false. As Timothy Williamson (1994, 124) notes, "A small degree of falsity in [the sorites's] conditional premises produces a high degree of falsity in its conclusion."

If validity is the preservation of perfect truth, then the argument is valid. If the inductive premise and the initial premise are true, then the conclusion must be true. If, on the other hand, validity is the preservation of degree of truth, then the argument might be thought invalid, because the degree of truth of one premise is greater than the degree of truth of the conclusion.

2.4.2 Concerns for the Fuzzy Logician

Imagine an orange-red patch of color that is exactly on the border between red and orange, that is, half red and half orange. If someone describes the patch by saying "This patch is red," then that person's utterance is 0.5-true. And the utterance "This patch is not red" is 0.5-true, as well. This is intuitive because a patch that is half-red, but not fully red, would, it seems, be half-not-red, as well. A question, however, arises with the utterance "This patch is red and this patch is not red." On the fuzzy account, an utterance of this conjunction has a truth-value of 0.5, because the truth-value of a conjunction is that of its lowest conjunct (see table 5). But this truth-value is counterintuitive; such a conjunction seems completely false, because both a statement and its denial are being asserted. To claim that this conjunction not perfectly false is to abandon the law of noncontradiction, which holds that statements and their denials cannot be true at the same time. Moreover, on the fuzzy account, the disjunction "This patch is red or this patch is not red" would also be 0.5-true because the truth-value of a disjunction, such as *P or Q*, is that of its greatest disjunct, in this case whichever is the greater of *P* or *Q* (see table 5). The truth-value of this disjunction is counterintuitive, because such a disjunction is logically true if one does not deny the law of the excluded middle.

In "Truth, Belief, and Vagueness," fuzzy logician Kenton Machina acknowledges the counterintuitive nature of fuzzy logic's treatment of conjunctions and disjunctions such as the previous example:

> It would seem that the most natural sort of truth-functional definitions of the connectives "v" and "&" in our multi-valued logic are likely to result in the loss of both the law of noncontradiction and the law of the excluded middle. Indeed, this is exactly what happens in the logic for which I shall argue. I take it that the loss of these laws may seem initially to be a sufficient ground for rejecting my approach; my strategy will be to try to make the loss seem appropriate and welcome. It happens that one can give up these laws without destroying logic; in fact in a sense it even turns out that these laws are preserved in the system to be described below— although they will not always be completely true, they will always be at least half-true. (1976, 56–57)

Machina claims that the loss of the laws of noncontradiction and excluded middle is "appropriate" and should be welcomed, because vagueness makes it appropriate to both assert and deny a statement. However, as Linda

Burns (1991, 60) has claimed in her book *Vagueness*, the possibility for being unreasonable would be severely limited if it were possible to both assert and deny the same statement. To assert a statement, it seems, is to assert its truth, and to deny a statement is to deny its truth. The person who does both at the same time is being unreasonable, yet under fuzzy logic this person may not be unreasonable at all. It is hard to see how anyone could be unreasonable if it were reasonable to both assert and deny the same statement at the same time.

Rohit Parikh (1994, 525) poses another question: "[Fuzzy logic] does not tell us why there should be *disagreements*. If someone is 0.5-bald, one might suppose that it would be possible to agree about *that*" (italics in original). In other words, in attempting to resolve disagreement and uncertainty about who should be classified as bald, the fuzzy logician merely moves the disagreement to particular degrees of baldness. There is no more agreement about 0.40-baldness than there is about baldness in general. In fact, there would seem to be more disagreement about 0.40-baldness than baldness in general.

2.4.3   General Analysis of You-Can't-Get-There-from-Here

As a strategy for solving paradoxes, the You-Can't -Get-There-From-Here solution works well when there is some easily exposed error in reasoning that makes the argument invalid. When such is not the case, which is true of the vast majority of paradoxes, the strategy relies on rejecting classical logical notions, such as validity, and replacing these notions with alternatives. The solution, then, is just as successful as its proposed alternate logic. As seen in the case of the fuzzy logic and the sorites, rejecting the reasoning involved in the sorites paradox using the fuzzy truth conditions may lead to a number of additional puzzles, so the supposed benefit of solving the paradox comes at too great a cost to our ordinary ideas of entailment.

Again, as with the preemptive strike, lowering our subjective probability about one part of the paradox leads to the proposed acceptance of other statements with lower subjective probabilities.

2.5   Solution-Type 4: The It's-All-Good Approach, Or Arguing that All the Parts of the Paradox Are Fine, Including a Counterintuitive Conclusion

Yet another common strategy for solving paradoxes is to show that the conclusion of the paradoxical argument, though seemingly false, is in fact true. The task then is to show why the conclusion is acceptable, despite all appearances to the contrary. We began this chapter with the Monty Hall paradox, which ultimately was solved by showing that the conclusion is indeed true. Though it runs counter to our intuitions, the contestant on the game show has better chance of winning the car by switching than by staying with her first choice. This is a classic It's-All-Good approach to a paradox. Although it looks as if the contestant is just as likely to win regardless of whether she switches, switching is the better option. All of the assumptions in the paradox are consistent, and although it is surprising that switching is the better option, it turns out that it is. And if we think of a paradox not as an argument, but as a set of mutually inconsistent statements, each of which seems true, the It's-All-Good solution attempts to show that there is really no mutual inconsistency among the statements in the paradox. They can all consistently be maintained at the same time, claims the It's-All-Good would-be solution.

2.5.1 A Systematic It's-All-Good Solution: Dialetheism, Paraconsistent Logic, and the Liar

Another It's-All-Good solution to a paradox is the account of the liar paradox given by dialetheism, the view that some contradictions are, in fact, true. Dialetheism has an interesting take on the liar paradox. Each of the first three sentences has high subjective probability. Yet, when taken together, they are mutually inconsistent, as is shown by the fact that they lead to the fourth statement:

Yet another common strategy for solving paradoxes is to show that the conclusion of the paradoxical argument, though seemingly false, is in fact true.

Box 16

The liar paradox

L: This sentence is false.

1. If (L) is true, then (L) is false.

2. If (L) is false, then (L) is true.

3. All sentences are either true or false (bivalence).

4. Therefore, (L) is both true and false.

By the dialetheist account, the conjunction of both the liar sentence and its denial (L & ~L) can be accepted as true. This issue is typically thought to be troubling because contradictions, if taken to be true, can be used to prove that anything is true. To mitigate this problem, the dialetheist uses a paraconsistent logic, which abandons some very intuitive logic principles, such as disjunctive syllogism, but allows for the truth of contradiction without entailing trivialism (the view that every statement is true).

Paraconsistent logic is a branch of logic that differs from classical logical and most nonclassical logics in its treatment of contradiction. Intuitively, when we find that a series of assumptions leads to contradiction, we think something has gone wrong. Contradictions (e.g., *P & not P*) are typically thought to be problematic for most logics.

In our everyday lives, if someone asserts something (e.g., *I have a blue car*) and then without explanation its denial (e.g., *I don't have a blue car*), our natural response is to think that something is wrong. We do not see this person as a reliable source of information. In classical logic, too, when a series of assumptions leads to a contradiction, logicians typically look back at the proof to see whether a mistake has been made. Part of this worry about contradiction is due to that fact that in classical logic, if we assume a contradiction, then we can derive anything. Here is an example of a logical argument that just pulls something "out of the air," as it were, and proves it using a contradiction. Let's say that we want to prove the claim r. We don't even have to define r, but for fun let's say that it refers to the claim *Zeno of Elea was a New Yorker*. Given any contradiction, we can prove r using classical logic. For example, take the contradiction *a & not a*, and let's define *a* as *Aristotle was a Macedonian*. So in our proof, we start with the contradiction that claims that Aristotle was a Macedonian and that it is not the case that Aristotle was a Macedonian. To symbolize this, let's call this claim *a & not a,* where & represents conjunction. This line then reads "a and not a." If we have this as an assumption, we can derive a couple obvious things. The first is *a*, and the second is *not a*. In other words, if *a and not a* is assumed, we then can derive, individually, *a*, and also *not a*. To give a little proof, we have the following:

Box 17

Proof using a contradiction

1. a & not a (assumption)
2. a (from 1, & elimination)
3. not a (from 1, & elimination)
4. a ∨ r (2, ∨I)
5. r (3, 4 Dis Syl)

Here, 2 and 3 follow from 1, because that is just the meaning of the & symbol. If *P&Q* is true, then *P* must be true and *Q* must be true, too. The parentheses list the lines of the proof and the rule from classical logic that allows us to derive the present line. Now, we can form an *or* statement, otherwise known as a *disjunction*. Let's take premise 2 (a) and form a disjunction with any random or crazy thing we want to prove. This approach is licensed by the meaning of the *or*, and symbolized by ∨. As long as you have one true statement, such as *Aristotle was a Macedonian*, then you are licensed to form an *or* statement such as *Aristotle was a Macedonian OR Zeno was a New Yorker*. This statement is written as *a ∨ r (2, ∨ I)*. The *(2, ∨ I)* just means that we are introducing an *or* statement, using the *a* from line 2 of the previous proof. Next, we can use the rule called *disjunctive syllogism*, which holds that if you have an *or* statement, and the denial of one part of the statement, then you can conclude the other part of it:

Box 18

Disjunctive syllogism

p or q
not q
therefore, p

In other words, if an *or* statement is true, then at least one of the two sides of the *or* has to be true. So, if the *denial* of one side is true, then the other side must be true. Assume the statement *I am left-handed or I am right-handed* is true. Also assume that it's not the case that I'm right-handed. We can then conclude that I am left-handed. Using this rule in our little proof, we then get to prove that Zeno was a New Yorker.

So, that's our proof that Zeno was a New Yorker. We can replace the *r* with any other statement and derive the same thing. All we did was assume a contradiction (a & not a), take out each side of it individually (*a*, plus *not a*), then create an *or* statement (*a v r*) using any random statement *r* that we wanted, and derive *r* because *a*'s denial (*not a*) was the case. What this proof shows, then, is that when you have a contradiction (e.g., *a & not a*), you can use a basic way of reasoning (e.g., disjunctive syllogism) to prove any statement. That's not a good thing, because if you can prove anything, your conclusions are trivial. If you can prove absolutely anything, the value of the things that are proven is completely weakened. That anything can be proven from classical logic when there is a contradiction means that classical logic is what is called *explosive*.

Paraconsistent logic allows for there to be contradictions within a logical system but restricts certain rules of logic so that it is not possible to conclude anything and everything from these contradictions; it is thus called *nonexplosive*. It also treats inconsistent statements such as *a & not a* as informative.

Paraconsistent logic provides an interesting way to handle arguments such as the one generated by the liar sentence, *This sentence is not true*, claiming that the contradiction in the conclusion that the sentence is both true and not true is not as worrisome as we think it is, because contradictions need not lead to everything being true. Once you get rid of disjunctive syllogism, the rule used to derive *Zeno was a New Yorker*, then contradictions cannot be used to prove any claim is true.

2.5.2   Reflections on Dialetheism and Paraconsistent Logic

Contradictions naturally inspire concern in those who detect them. When paradoxes arise, attempts are made at solution, indicating that contradictions among the very intuitive parts of the paradoxes pose some kind of problem and that a return to consistency is a good thing. Although I am in agreement that we must somehow learn to live with a certain degree of contradiction among our beliefs, especially those beliefs that involve our ordinary language concepts such as *truth*, *knowledge*, *beauty*, and so on, to say that contradictions can fall under the banner of truth, it seems, attempts to legitimize them in a way that doesn't take seriously enough the problems they raise. Also, I'm not sure that the sentence *L is true and not true* being itself true really solves the underlying problem that leads to the paradox. For example, how would such an account handle the sentences *L is only not true* or *L is only false*? It seems the problem returns when the liar sentence is altered slightly.

2.5.3   "An Extravagant Paradox or Palpable Absurdity": The Paradox of Taste, and a Supervaluationist It's-All-Good Solution

[1] To seek the real beauty, or real deformity is as fruitless an inquiry, as to pretend to ascertain the real sweet or real bitter. According to the disposition of the

organs, the same object may be both sweet and bitter; and the proverb has justly determined it to be fruitless to dispute concerning tastes. It is very natural, and even quite necessary, to extend this axiom to mental, as well as bodily taste; and thus common sense, which is so often at variance with philosophy, especially with the sceptical kind, is found, in one instance at least, to agree in pronouncing the same decision. . . . [2] Whoever would assert an equality of genius and elegance between Ogilby and Milton, or Bunyan and Addison, would be thought to defend no less an extravagance, than if he had maintained a mole-hill to be as high as Teneriffe, or a pond as extensive as the ocean. Though there may be found persons, who give the preference to the former authors; no one pays attention to such a taste; and we pronounce, without scruple, the sentiment of these pretended critics to be absurd and ridiculous.

—David Hume, "Of the Standard of Taste"

Scottish philosopher David Hume is credited with proposing what is known as the *paradox of taste*. Put as a set of mutually inconsistent statements, each of which seems true, the paradox is phrased simply as two claims, first that (1) *there is no disputing matters of taste* and the second that (2) *we are capable of distinguishing good from bad works of art*. Both statements (1) and (2) are described in the selections from Hume's "Of the Standard of Taste" that begin this section. If, in fact, matters of taste are completely subjective, then it seemingly makes no sense to even attempt to distinguish good art from bad art. Yet we do this all the time, and in a seemingly conclusive way. How can these two inconsistent statements both be true?

Hume's It's-All-Good solution argues that both are true, under special interpretations of the words *sentiment* and *taste*. Maybe we can't dispute the fact that someone doesn't like a work, or has a negative reaction to it, but we can claim, for example, that this person is wrong in thinking that his or her sentiment is reflective of the true nature of the work. For Hume, "All sentiment is right; because sentiment has a reference to nothing beyond itself, and is always real, wherever a man is conscious of it. But all determinations of the understanding are not right; because they have a reference to something beyond themselves, to wit, real matter of fact" (1757, 8–9). In fact, he goes even further, claiming, "Beauty is no quality in things themselves: It exists merely in the mind which contemplates them; and each mind perceives a different beauty" (9). Seeking the real beauty, for Hume, would be like seeking the real spicy. What is spicy to one tongue may be bland to another. Yet when we compare two works, such as an ice cream truck tune to a Bach fugue, an "extravagant paradox, or rather a palpable absurdity arises" (9) in which there is no objective standard for the claim that the latter is more beautiful than the former.

To resolve this extravagant paradox, Hume claims that although the former statement—that there is no disputing the sentiments regarding a work of art—is indubitable, there must be some standard, based on experience—that is, based on "general observations, concerning what has been universally found to please in all countries and in all ages" (9). So although we cannot deny that there are different sentiments regarding what is beautiful or not, we can deny that these sentiments conform to "universally" accepted ideas of what is pleasing or not. To flesh out the second statement, Hume emphasizes that our sentiments regarding the beautiful, like our other faculties, can be cultivated by practice, claiming that, "though there be naturally a wide difference in point of delicacy between one person and another, nothing tends further to increase and improve this talent, than practice in a particular art, and the frequent survey or contemplation of a particular species of beauty . . . the same address and dexterity, which practice gives to the execution of any work, is also acquired by the same means, in the judging of it" (13).

If Hume is right in this, and our faculties of taste can be perfected, then although we cannot deny that a person doesn't have the experience of beauty when listening to a Bach fugue, we can say that his or her faculty for perceiving beauty may not be able to discern the properties that, if experienced, would give rise to this experience. Just as the novice guitarist thinks that all guitars are the same because he or she doesn't perceive the subtle differences between guitars, but later comes to be an expert at noticing subtle distinctions and fine points after practice, someone with a finely developed faculty will be better able to adjudicate among different works of art, because the person with the more developed faculty will be better able to discern the properties in nature that give rise to the true experience of beauty.

So, although beauty exists in the mind alone, there are certain properties in nature that give rise to it in those who have the capacity for experiencing nature correctly. Part of the development of this faculty for experiencing beauty, for Hume, involves being delicate, that is, being able to experience subtle differences among comparable works and small details. Practice, as discussed earlier, is important as well: freeing oneself of prejudice, especially with regard to fashion, must be done, but not at the expense of understanding that not every custom is a good one. Hume, for example, says, "Must we throw aside the pictures of our ancestors, because of their ruffs and hooped skirts? But where the ideas of morality and decency alter from one age to another, and where vicious manners are described, without being marked with the proper characters of blame and disapprobation, this must be allowed to disfigure the poem, and to be a real deformity" (1757, 18). Some of the jokes, for example, of television shows as beloved as the classic *The Honeymooners*, with the hapless husband Ralph

Kramden shaking his fist at his wife, and threatening her with "Bam, zoom, right to the moon, Alice!" strike a more observant viewer as abusive and hardly a laughing matter. Finally, there is good sense, or the ability to reason effectively (15). These are activities that develop our aesthetic sense and make us better able to discern the beautiful.

So the paradox of taste is resolved by claiming that both claims 1 and 2 are true. We cannot adjudicate among diverse sentiments of taste. We can, however, point to universal features of objects that, through experience of different ages and cultures, have been universally acknowledged to elicit pleasurable sentiments in those with highly cultivated faculties for experiencing the beautiful. We can then say that one person's sentiments may not be as accurate a gauge of the relationship between the properties of nature that give rise to feelings of pleasure or displeasure in a work of art.

What, then, of the possibility of two persons, with equally developed faculties for perceiving the beautiful, who have different perceptions of what is beautiful and what is not? Is this possible for Hume? Hume claims that this is in some way unavoidable, for "it is plainly an error in a critic, to give his approval to one sort or style of writing and condemn all the rest. But it is almost impossible not to feel some inclination in favor of the sort or style that suits our particular temperamant and character. Such preferences are harmless and unavoidable, and it is never reasonable to argue about them because there is no standard by which they can be decided" (1757, 17). But this sounds more like admitting that except for cases in which there is a consensus among experts, there is no resolving the paradox. Hume's response might thus be seen to resemble a Facing-the-Music solution, in which the paradox is treated as unavoidable. Despite having solved the paradox for the more obvious disputes, there still remains the question of whether two equally developed moral senses could have different takes on the same work. The answer, for Hume, is *yes*. If we are to take this resolution as an It's-All-Good approach, we have to acknowledge that it fails. If, on the other hand, Hume's admission that two equally good judges can have divergent opinions on a work's beauty, we are left again with the question of whether a correct view exists among these two opinions. Perhaps we can resolve this issue with a slight revision to the second statement, that we are capable of distinguishing *some* good art from bad art. In cases where there is no general consensus among equally developed senses, then we cannot, but in other cases where there is such a consensus, we can.

One way to flesh this issue out using a contemporary logic known as *supervaluationism* is to take a range of admissible interpretations; let's call them *valuations* (van Fraassen 1966). Each valuation will assign truth or falsity to claims about an object's aesthetic value. A valuation is admissible if it conforms to the guidelines mentioned by Hume—delicacy, practice, freedom from prejudice, and good sense—and conforms to other standards for admissibility specified by the supervaluationist logic. By stipulation, an interpretation is *admissible* if it respects all ostensive and theoretical connections. Respect for theoretical and observational connections is needed in order to avoid conflict with experience and the specifications of other terms; for example, an interpretation that treated the term *beautiful* as referring to a particular object must not also treat the term *ugly* as applying to the same object.

When confronted with the statement *Leonardo da Vinci's* Mona Lisa *is beautiful*, some acceptable valuations will assign this statement truth, and others may (or may not) assign this statement falsity. If all the acceptable valuations are in agreement that the statement is true, then we can assign the claim the supervaluation "super-true" to the statement *Leonardo da Vinci's* Mona Lisa *is beautiful*, but if there is some dissension among the acceptable valuations, then although it is true for some interpretations and false for others, we cannot claim that the statement is super-true or true on all acceptable interpretations. Likewise, if all acceptable valuations assign falsity to the statement that some work *x* is beautiful, then the statement *x is beautiful* is assigned the value "super-false." This approach allows for disagreements among equally acceptable valuation systems but also allows that some super-values may bind the different acceptable valuations together. Thus, the supervaluationist way of solving the paradox of taste holds that although it may be that adjudicating among matters of taste is not possible, we can, using supervaluationism, still determine objectively whether some artwork is good or bad.

Of course, the success of a supervaluationist solution to the paradox of taste depends on whether it avoids other problematic results. If, for example, only one admissible interpretation classifies *x is beautiful* as true, while thousands of others classify *x is beautiful* as false, then should we think of the statement *x is beautiful* as being almost super-false? Or assign it the realm of false on most interpretations, but true on one? One might wonder whether consensus, even among "admissible" interpretations, is enough to solve the paradox.

2.5.4 General Analysis of the It's-All-Good Solution-Type

As a strategy for solving paradoxes, the It's-All-Good solution-type proceeds by trying to reconcile intuitively irreconcilable parts of the paradox. In most cases, it tries to say that there is no internal contradiction among the parts of the paradox. If we take the definition of *paradox* as a set of mutually inconsistent statements, each of which seems true, this solution-type attempts to show that the parts are not mutually inconsistent after all. And according to the definition of *paradox* as an argument with seemingly true premises, apparently correct reasoning, and an obviously false or contradictory conclusion, the strategy shows that the conclusion isn't really false at all.

The success, or failure, of such a solution then hinges on how successfully it is able to show that the conclusion of the paradoxical argument is in fact true, or that the seemingly inconsistent propositions turn out to be all true and consistent. As has been shown, although a weaker paradox (such as the Monty Hall paradox) might admit of such a solution, the stronger ones (such as the liar paradox) are not so easily treated.

2.6   Solution-Type 5: The Detour: Creating Alternative Notions

The Detour is the first solution-type I'll discuss that doesn't try to lower the subjective probability of one part of the paradox. Each part of the paradox, according to this solution-type, has strong intuitive force because each part of the paradox accurately represents some feature of the concepts that lead to the paradox. The strategy is to acknowledge that the concepts themselves lead to paradox, and the only way to avoid paradox is to provide a replacement concept. Doing so does not remove the paradox, grants the proponent of a Detour solution. Yet a replacement concept that closely mimics the original notion in the most relevant ways and does not lead to the paradox, claims the user of the Detour solution, can be given.

2.6.1 Tarski's Detour from the Liar, Grelling's, and Definability Paradoxes

In "The Semantic Conception of Truth and the Foundations of Semantics," Alfred Tarski (1944) gives a diagnosis of why the liar paradox arises. For Tarski, the trouble with statements such as *What I am now saying is false* arises because natural languages such as English, Spanish, and so on, are semantically closed. That is, the expressions of the language are used to describe the language itself. Expressions like *is true, is false, is a sentence* are both part of the language and used to describe the language at the same time. Like the famous M. C. Escher print of two hands in which each hand depicted in the drawing is drawing the other, the things that are created by something—in this case, the expressions of a language—are used to give a picture of the language itself. English, for example, does not distinguish between that language being used by the speakers of the language (what Tarski calls *the object language*) and that language that talks about the language itself (what Tarski calls the *metalanguage*). Our ordinary use of the word *true* provides ample evidence of how a word in the language, *true*, is used in talking about other parts of the language, as in the sentence *What she said was true*.

While acknowledging this, Tarski proposed another way of thinking about truth, involving something he terms *satisfaction* and using a semantically open language, one in which there are different hierarchies of sublanguages and no one sublanguage will describe itself. Satisfaction is a relation between objects, on the one hand, and sentential functions such as *x is a nephew* on the other. Sentential functions take the form of regular sentences, except for containing free variables such as *x*. Once the free variable is replaced by an object—say, the name of a person—the expression is simply a sentence, as in "Anthony is a nephew." A sentence is true, for Tarski (1944, 353), "if it is satisfied by all objects and false if it is satisfied by no objects."

Satisfaction is a recursive notion; in other words, more complex sentential functions are built out of simpler ones. For example, two objects, *x* and *y*, satisfy "*x* is lesser or equal to *y*" if they satisfy either "*x* is lesser than *y*" or "*x* is equal to *y*." More precisely, a recursive definition gives rules for figuring out what counts as a member of the set of the thing defined, using a base case, and then building up repeatedly (i.e., recursively) from that case. For example, here's a recursive definition of *even number* for non-negative numbers. A member of the set of non-negative integers is in the set of even numbers if, and only if, given that 0 is an even number (base case), this number + 2 is in the set of even numbers. As this example illustrates, a recursive definition can be repeated for all potential members of the set. Given that 0 is a member of the set of even numbers, by adding 2 we can churn out all even numbers.

The alternative notion of truth that Tarski proposes has the goal of meeting two criteria. First it will be *materially adequate*: it will conform to our everyday notions of truth. Specifically, according to this notion, every sentence of the form *"p" is true if, and only if p* turns out to be true. Tarski calls this concept *Convention T*. Convention T requires that any statement described in a language (i.e., in quotes or italics) be true just in case, when the statement is not described but actually used, it is true. So "Snow is white" is true if, and only if, snow is white. This convention is symbolized as follows:

Box 19

Tarski's Convention T

"φ" is true, if and only if φ

So the sentence *grass is green* will be true when, and only when, grass is green. And *grass is orange* will be true if, and only if, grass is indeed orange. Because grass is not orange, the sentence will not be true. But it would be true in the event that grass were indeed orange. The second condition is that the definition of truth must be formally correct, which means that it must not be circular and must be consistent. The notion cannot lead to contradiction if it is going to be formally correct.

2.6.2 Tarski's Detour around the Paradox

Because Tarski's account of truth employs the distinction between object and metalanguages, the sentence *This sentence is false* turns out to be problematic because it mixes up the distinction. It both uses the language (object language) and describes it (metalanguage) at the same time. Tarski's replacement notion of truth, satisfaction, doesn't do this. It also gives us what we want in a definition of truth; namely, it is materially adequate so that every sentence of the form *"p" is true if, and only if, p* turns out true, and it is formally correct so that the definition doesn't lead to contradiction or circularity.

For Tarski, this is true as well for other semantic paradoxes, that is, paradoxes having to do with meaning and truth, including Grelling's paradox, and the definability paradox. Because we haven't discussed these earlier, it will be helpful to examine Grelling's and the definability paradoxes briefly.

Grelling's paradox concerns the word *heterological*, which refers to words that are not true of their own names. The word *homological*, on the other hand, refers to words that are true of their own names. For example, the word *short* is a short word, so it is homological. The word *long*, on the other hand, is not a long word, so it is not true of its own name, and is heterological. But now a question arises about the status of the word *heterological*. Is the word heterological itself? If the word *heterological* is indeed heterological, then it wouldn't be true of its own name. But *being a word that isn't true of its own name* is precisely the definition of *heterological*. So, it would be heterological. So if the word is heterological, then it is homological. And if the word is homological, then it refers to itself. Because heterological words do not apply to themselves, it applies to itself if, and only if, it does not apply to itself.

Also, a definability paradox is one in which a term or concept is defined in a way that leads to contradiction. For example, let *A* be the set of all positive integers that can be defined in fewer than 100 words. Because there are only finitely many of these, there must be a smallest positive integer *n* that does not belong to A. But this number can be defined as the "smallest positive integer *n* that does not belong to A" and is hence defined in fewer than 100 words. So, it should belong to A. So this number, it seems, both belongs to A and does not.

As with the liar, Tarski's approach to Grelling's and the definability paradoxes does away with the common ordinary language notion of truth, replacing it with the less troubling notion of satisfaction. This notion adheres to the distinction between hierarchies in languages, in which one sublanguage does not refer to itself. It is, however, not without problems. Saul Kripke (1975) pointed out that we often encounter pairs of sentences in which one sentence is saying something about the other. For example, imagine that a reporter says of the disgraced and imprisoned Bernard Madoff, "All of Madoff's claims about his investment company are false," and Madoff responds, "Everything that reporter said about my investment company is false." By Tarski's account, there is something wrong with both statements, because each violates the metalanguage/object language distinction. Yet as Kripke claims, we often not only understand such claims but can assign truth-values to them. Tarski, though, might respond that he is not concerned about natural languages, so such a problem is irrelevant. Still, such situations do raise questions about how closely Tarski's account mirrors the natural language notion of truth.

2.6.3 Analysis of the Detour as a Solution-Type

The Detour solution-type does nothing to lower the subjective probability of a part of the paradox. Instead, it tries to create an alternative notion in which there are no sets of assumptions that each have high subjective probabilities that are in conflict. A natural response to this solution-type is that although it avoids some troubling consequences brought out by the paradox, it does nothing to address the paradox itself. It thus falls prey to the claim that its treatment of the paradox in question is ad hoc and does not fully address the problems raised by the paradox.

2.7 Solution-Type 6: Facing the Music: Accepting the Paradox

Some solutions say that the paradox exposes a way in which our concepts are flawed and that nothing can be done to resolve this conflict.

2.7.1 A Facing-the-Music Solution to the Dollar Cost Auction

Imagine that two players are each given a $2.50 bankroll and offered a dollar in an auction-type sale. The dollar goes to the highest bidder, no matter how high or low the bid is. In this game, though, the second highest bidder also pays the amount of his or her bid and gets nothing. The game allows bids in increments of 5 cents. If this game allows co-operation, then the optimal strategy is for the first player to offer 5 cents and the second to not bid. The two players would then divide the 95-cent profit. If, on the other hand, no cooperation is allowed, then the optimal strategy is for the first player to make a bid that is a function of the player's bankroll and the stakes of the game, and for the second player to not bid. For example, if the bankroll of the first player is $2.50 and bids are set to a minimum of 5 cents per bid, the first player should bid 60 cents and the other player should stay out. (The solution to the problem, according to O'Neill [1986], is given in a game tree with

Some solutions say that
the paradox exposes
a way in which our
concepts are flawed
and that nothing can be
done to resolve this
conflict.

about 2,500 branches.) Suffice it to say that normal human beings cannot make such decisions in the moment and the most rational strategy is thus to not enter the game at all.

If, however, the game is entered into by at least two players, then the unintended escalation starts and is a direct consequence of a reasonable process of reasoning. Assume that we have a front-runner who has bid $1.00 and a runner-up who has bid 95 cents. The runner-up is about to lose 95 cents; the way to avoid this loss is to bid $1.05, so that this person will "win" and lose only 5 cents. Of course, the person who bid $1.00 would then want to cut his or her losses in the same way, so his or her bid would be raised to $1.10. Loss of 10 cents is preferable to loss of $1.00 to this person. And so on. The process continues until one player's money is exhausted.

According to Moaz (1990), in practice players typically enter the game and the pattern of play is one of infinite escalation. (My own experience is a little different.) Starting with very small bids, play slows down around the $1.00 range and then goes past the $1.00 range, ending with the person who has the second largest bankroll exhausting his or her money. In actuality, the game has no winner, the second-highest bidder has lost everything, and the "winner" has paid far more for the dollar than it is worth. Both parties would have been better off if the game had ended sooner, yet each move in the game was justified.

According to Costanza, the "only truly rational thing to do is not enter the game in the first place. Once the game is entered by at least two bidders, their fate is sealed if they behave rationally from that point on" (Maoz 1990, 221). Yet, according to O'Neill, "if you know your opponent would not bid you should clearly make some small bid. Thus, if the rational strategy for both is not to play and if you know your opponent is rational, then you can deduce that the rational strategy for you is to play, which is a contradiction" (Maoz 1990, 221).

To put the paradox succinctly, once the play begins, each step in the escalation of the bids is rationally justified. Yet this strategy leads to both players "losing" in the end. However, if the other player knows that the player's opponent won't enter the bidding, the player should make the lowest bid on the dollar. Once the dollar auction has begun, each individual play in the game is rational; yet, when taken as a whole, the process leads to a worse outcome for both players. And it is irrational to engage in such a process. So each of the individual steps in the game is in the player's interest, yet the total strategy is against it.

The paradox can be applied to two nations going to war. In this case, usually, the "game" has been entered. According to Moaz, "Recklessness is the consequence of perfectly reasonable calculations involving the notion that escalation is perfectly controllable because war is something that nobody wants. Each side believes that it can frighten the opponent by manipulating the risks of war. But when the parties reach the threshold of war, they cannot back down because nobody can afford to become the loser" (1990, 110). Moaz also states: "Crises may escalate precisely because politicians are reasonable and prudent and precisely because they do all in their power to avoid confrontation. In a system of interactions where what one gets depends as much on what other actors do as on what one does, things may get out of hand precisely *because* each side tries to prevent them from getting out of hand" (103–104).

The reasoning used in the paradox of crisis escalation may strike some as similar to the sorites paradox. The individual moves in the game can be thought of as employing something like the second premise in the sorites paradox. Each of the individual moves seems to be warranted. Similarly, each step in a sorites series of, for example, hairs on one's head seems licensed. If a person with 100 hairs is bald, then it seems that a person with 101 would have to be bald as well, because the difference of one hair is so small. Likewise, each of the individual moves in the dollar auction, once begun, is completely rational. Yet the overall outcome, as in the sorites paradox, is unacceptable.

One response to this paradox is to say that the paradox of crisis escalation cannot be solved. That is, we might accept the paradox as showing that there are certain situations in which our reasoning about the best course of action does not work. Such a solution—an example of a

Facing-the-Music solution to a paradox—might seem like a cop-out. Rather than rolling up one's sleeves and finding a solution, this type of approach says that no solution can be given. A more thoroughgoing Facing-the-Music solution would not merely say that there is no solution but explain why this so. In his book *The Things We Mean*, Stephen Schiffer (2003) calls this type of solution an *unhappy-face solution* to a paradox. The solution not only says that there can be no successful solution, but also says why this is so.

2.7.2 Michael Dummett's Solution to the Sorites Paradox

Another, more thorough example of a Facing-the-Music solution is Michael Dummett's solution to the sorites paradox. In "Wang's Paradox," Michael Dummett (1975) describes a second feature of vagueness, one that is similar to tolerance. He calls this feature of observational predicates the *nontransitivity of nondiscriminable difference*. Dummett claims (1975, 314) that "the dropping of one grain of sand could not make the difference between what was not and what is a heap—not just because we have not chosen to draw a sharp line between what is and what is not a heap, but because there would be no difference which could be discerned by observation." Non-discriminable difference is nontransitive, because even though one grain could not make the difference, fifty or so such grains eventually could. If, for example, I ask someone to put a heap of salt on a plate and the person puts one grain, then he has not complied with my request. If he puts one more, he has still not complied, yet by doing this repeatedly he will have done what I asked him to do. By pointing to the nontransitivity of the relation "not discriminably different," Dummett describes one striking feature of vagueness: although there is a degree of change that makes no difference (tolerance), eventually the minute degrees add up to something that does make a difference. Dummett describes the following scenario:

> I look at something which is moving, but moving too slowly for me to be able to see that is moving. After one second, it still looks to me as though it was in the same position; similarly after three seconds. After four seconds, however, I can recognize that it has moved from where it was at the start, i.e. four seconds ago. At this time, however, it does not look to me as though it is in a different position from that which it was in one, or even three seconds before. (1975, 316)

In this scenario, the person cannot discern anything less than the distance traveled in four seconds. So the person, despite being capable of seeing that the object has moved from its original position, cannot see that the object has moved from where it was a second ago or even three seconds ago. Based upon the previous example, Dummett claims that the person contradicts himself in the attempt to express how the object looks:

> Suppose I give the name "position X" to the position in which I first see it, and make an announcement every second. Then at the end of the first second, I must say, "It still looks to me to be in position X." And I must say the same at the end of the second and the third second. What am I to say at the end of the fourth second? It does not seem that I can say anything other than, "It no longer looks to me to be in position X": for position X was defined to be the position it was when I first started looking at it, and, by hypothesis, at the end of four seconds it no longer looks to me to be in the same position as when I started looking. But then, it seems that, from the fact that after three seconds I said, "It still looks to me to be in position X," that I am committed to the proposition, "After four seconds it looks to me to be in a different position from that it was in after three seconds." But this is precisely what I want to deny. (1975, 316)

The person judging the position of the object is both constrained after four seconds to judge the present position of the object as being different from that of position X and constrained to say that the object looks to be in a different position than it was three seconds ago. Yet the person is not able to discern a difference after three seconds.

From the previous example, Dummett concludes that vague predicates are "intrinsically inconsistent" (1975, 319), and the sorites paradox reflects this inconsistency. "What is in error is not the principles of reasoning involved, nor, as on our earlier diagnosis, the induction step. The induction step is correct, according to the rules of the use governing vague predicates such as 'small': but these rules are themselves inconsistent, and hence the paradox. Our earlier model for the logic of vague expressions thus becomes useless: there can be no coherent such logic" (1975, 319–320).

2.7.3 Analysis of the Facing-the-Music Solution-Type

By explaining the paradox and how no straightforward solution can be attained, such a "solution" does not reduce our subjective probability about one part of the paradox. It merely shows how the internal conflict arises and why the parts of the paradox have the subjective probabilities they have.

One natural response to this type of so-called solution is that it is not really a solution at all. It doesn't solve anything, but it acknowledges the paradox. The point of solutions, claims this type of criticism, is to show how something in a paradox is mistaken. This type of criticism assumes that the purpose of a solution is to show that the paradox isn't as troubling as it seems. As you'll see in the next section, this type of assumption about solutions—which dates at least to Aristotle—may in fact be too optimistic about the underlying coherence of our ordinary folk concepts.

2.8   Which Solution-Types to Use, and When

This section is likely more contentious than previous sections. Here I argue, controversially, that as the paradoxicality of something increases, it becomes less and less likely that it admits of anything like the first four solution-types. The Preemptive-Strike, Odd-Guy-Out, You-Can't-Get-There-from-Here, and It's-All-Good solution-types seek to expose some type of flaw in the paradoxical argument, and to lower our subjective probability regarding that flawed part. For all but the most shallow of paradoxes, these strategies are unsuccessful. For the deepest of paradoxes, the more limited Detour and Facing-the-Music solution-types are the only viable options. These solution-types, though, are often subjected to the criticism that they are so restricted that they are not really solving the paradox at all.

An inductive argument for this claim follows in chapter 3, in which a survey of the history of solutions to paradoxes is given and a case is made that previous failures at attempting solution-types 1 through 4 are evidence that future such solutions are doomed to failure in most cases. Here, though, I present an argument based on the nature of the concepts that give rise to paradoxes. These concepts—ordinary natural-language "folk concepts" such as baldness, truth, knowledge, prediction, and so on—are the products, I submit, of our linguistic practices, practices that for the most part require a limited amount of precision, often admit of vagueness, and sometimes even admit of contradiction. To have more precise, less flawed folk concepts would require greater cognitive capacities than our species needs. And conflict among our beliefs is not an unusual or unnatural thing. In response to such conflicts, one belief is often rejected. However, in some cases, we are left with the awareness that there is no nonarbitrary way to resolve this difference. The first paragraph of William James's "What Pragmatism Means" nicely touches on this point:

> Some years ago, being with a camping party in the mountains, I returned from a solitary ramble to find every one engaged in a ferocious metaphysical dispute. The corpus of the dispute was a squirrel—a live squirrel supposed to be clinging to one side of a tree-trunk; while over against the tree's opposite side a human being was imagined to stand. This human witness tries to get sight of the squirrel

by moving rapidly round the tree, but no matter how fast he goes, the squirrel moves as fast in the opposite direction, and always keeps the tree between himself and the man, so that never a glimpse of him is caught. The resultant metaphysical problem now is this: *Does the man go round the squirrel or not?* He goes round the tree, sure enough, and the squirrel is on the tree; but does he go round the squirrel? In the unlimited leisure of the wilderness, discussion had been worn threadbare. Everyone had taken sides, and was obstinate; and the numbers on both sides were even. Each side, when I appeared therefore appealed to me to make it a majority. Mindful of the scholastic adage that whenever you meet a contradiction you must make a distinction, I immediately sought and found one, as follows: "Which party is right," I said, "depends on what you practically mean by 'going round' the squirrel. If you mean passing from the north of him to the east, then to the south, then to the west, and then to the north of him again, obviously the man does go round him, for he occupies these successive positions. But if on the contrary you mean being first in front of him, then on the right of him, then behind him, then on his left, and finally in front again, it is quite as obvious that the man fails to go round him, for by the compensating movements the squirrel makes, he keeps his belly turned towards the man all the time, and his back turned away. Make the distinction, and there is no occasion for any farther dispute. You are both right and both wrong according as you conceive the verb 'to go round' in one practical fashion or the other."

Although one or two of the hotter disputants called my speech a shuffling evasion, saying they wanted no quibbling or scholastic hair-splitting, but meant just plain honest English "round," the majority seemed to think that the distinction had assuaged the dispute. (1906/2008, 26)

Sometimes, our concepts such as *to go around* break down. They lack the specificity, or they contain inherent inconsistencies. Consider, too, the following list of concepts: I am willing to wager that you have an intuitive understanding of each of the folk concepts listed. Folk concepts are

Box 20

Sample folk concepts

baldness, liar, expectation, space, rationality, truth, falsity, pollution, knowledge, goodness, belief, time, intention, forgiveness, beauty, ugliness

---

the concepts that folks use in their everyday lives. Without them, we would surely be unable to function. Each folk concept in the previous list has given rise to at least one paradox, though—and not only shallow paradoxes, but ones, like the liar paradox, that have been around for millennia.

Some attempts to solve paradoxes, as we have seen, try to revise the folk concept with an alternative concept that doesn't lead to the paradox. I labeled these the Detour solutions to paradoxes, and said that examples of these types of solutions include Tarski's solution to the liar paradox. Such solutions, despite being useful in situations in which greater precision is needed, do not solve the paradox in the sense of keeping the basic folk concept. The Preemptive-Strike solutions reject the paradoxical notion as incoherent. In the case of folk concepts, though, it hardly makes sense to reject a concept that is so central to our everyday lives. Other solutions to paradoxes find fault not with the folk concepts, but with some assumption made by the paradox. These I called the Odd-Guy-Out solutions to paradoxes. These, we saw, work best when the paradox is a weak one, and a flaw easily seen. Still others— the You-Can't Get-There-from-Here solutions—question the reasoning in the paradox and leave the concept alone, and often rely on tweaking the way that we think about logical proof. In essence, the folk concept is kept at the expense of our ordinary intuitions about proving something. Still others, the It's-All-Good solutions, hold that the folk concepts don't give rise to such troubling consequences after all. Last, the Facing-the-Music solutions acknowledge the importance of the concepts, yet at the same time maintain that paradox cannot be avoided. Each solution-type, though, has little to offer in terms of easy solutions to the deepest of philosophical paradoxes.

When folk concepts are discussed, it is most usually in the context of cognitive science or moral psychology. Suspicions about psychological folk concepts such as *belief*, *think*, *fear*, and *prefer*, for example, and the controversies surrounding to what, if anything, these concepts refer, began at least as early as the dawn of a psychological theory known as *behaviorism*, which rejected these concepts as primitive notions that didn't have any basis in the physical world. As J. B. Watson famously said (1930, 3), concepts such as *belief* and *desire* are "heritages of a timid savage past," akin to concepts referring to magic. Such concepts have no place in scientific inquiry, according to this view. Instead, scientists should focus on phenomena that can be observed and tested, and this means behavior.

The lack of consensus among competing solutions to paradoxes suggests a similar conclusion about the other folk concepts. Although such concepts are useful for ordinary folk, they can easily be shown to lack precision and ultimately lead to contradiction. Whether it is our fundamental conception about what makes something beautiful, how much hair is needed for someone not to be bald, or what counts as real knowledge, if we test these concepts enough, we find ways in which they break down and lead to strongly counterintuitive results or downright contradiction. Do the conceptual glitches mean that the concepts are any less useful in ordinary situations? No. However, if—in extraordinary situations—the need for better concepts arises, replacement notions can do the work that the folk concepts can't do. Does this "solve" the paradoxes? No. Is this a huge problem? I don't see why.

2.9   Conclusion

Philosophical paradoxes have received countless pages of treatment by some of the best philosophers over thousands of years. The claim that such timeless problems lack all but the most restricted solution-type will strike many as an extremely pessimistic view about the philosophical enterprise. Philosophical paradoxes are about as old as philosophy itself and are like old friends to many philosophers, myself included. But, as Aristotle once said, we must prefer the truth to friends. Paradoxes often lack solution-types 1 through 4 because paradoxes expose conceptual glitches in the folk concepts that give rise to them. How, then, should paradoxes be solved? To best "solve" any but the most shallow of philosophical paradoxes requires accepting that they expose fundamental flaws in the concepts that lead to paradox. Alternative concepts may then be introduced, and these concepts may prevent some of the negative consequences that were implied by the original paradox, but there are no straightforward solutions in the sense of pointing to fallacies in the paradox. A system may be constructed according to which premises are false, conclusions true, or reasoning is invalid, but this construction involves creating a substitute concept different from the one that led to the paradox, and, ultimately, an acceptance of the paradox.

PARADOX LOST? ON THE SUCCESSES (AND FAILURES) OF SOLUTIONS TO PARADOXES

3.1 Introduction: Learning from History

> That no classical philosophical problem including the
> sorites [paradox] yet has a happy-face solution[1] is
> attested to by the fact that we are still debating each one.
> —Stephen Schiffer, *The Things We Mean*

An influential argument in the philosophy of science is
relevant to our discussion of paradoxes. It runs as follows:
throughout the long history of science, most scientific
theories have been proven false and the entities posited
by these theories were proven to not exist. Based on this
evidence from the past, it is rational to conclude that propositions of present (and future) scientific theories are false
and the entities posited by the theories nonexistent, as

well. Larry Laudan (1977) famously provided a long list of empirically successful theories—that is, generally accepted theories that could usually provide successful predictions—that were eventually rejected and their theoretical terms shown to not refer. The list includes the crystalline spheres of ancient and medieval astronomy, the humoral theory of medicine, the effluvial theory of static electricity, catastrophic geology and its commitment to a universal (Noachian) flood, the phlogiston theory of heat, the vibratory theory of heat, the vital force theory of physiology, the theory of circular inertia, theories of spontaneous generation, the optical ether theory, the electromagnetic ether theory, and many others.

This line of argument, called the *pessimistic meta-induction* argument, can be used to question not only realist theories of science which hold that the terms used by (true) scientific theories refer to real objects, but also other types of theory, including theories that provide would-be solutions to philosophical paradoxes. Take, as an example, ancient paradoxes such as the liar paradox. In the approximately 2,500 years since the liar paradox was first discussed, there have been countless attempts to provide a straightforward solution to it. And although each present-day advocate of a particular solution claims to have solved the paradox, it stubbornly refuses such solution.

Moreover, there is even more of a lack of consensus regarding solutions to paradoxes than there is regarding competing scientific theories. Given the vast amount of time and effort, and given that such solutions fare even worse than false scientific theories in terms of establishing a consensus and approximating a correct solution, the most rational attitude to take toward the deepest paradoxes is that they lack clear-cut solutions.

A pessimistic meta-induction does not provide reasons why paradoxes, qua paradoxes, lack solution-types 1 through 4. Nor could the conclusions drawn by this type of reasoning be decisive in the sense of a successful deductive proof. However, what such an argument does do is provide grounds for thinking that a particular research strategy is *probably* fruitless. Like other philosophical problems such as the mind-body problem, problems of personal identity, and others in the history of philosophy, the problems were not "solved" in a standard sense. The terms of the debate were changed. Does such an argument provide decisive grounds for rejecting solution-types 1 through 4 for all but the shallowest paradoxes? If by "decisive" we mean an exceedingly strong probability that such solutions will fail, then yes. If by "decisive" we mean "irrefutable logical proof," then no. But coupled with the conceptual argument presented at the end of chapter 2, it strikes me as exceedingly implausible to claim that the deepest paradoxes have such solutions. In this chapter, a pessimistic meta-induction argument is given for solutions to philosophical paradoxes by surveying the history of solutions to philosophical paradoxes.

Interestingly, pessimistic meta-induction provides a stronger case against there being solutions to philosophical paradoxes than against scientific realism. Some of the standard replies to pessimistic meta-induction's critique of scientific realism cannot be equally lodged against its application to solutions to philosophical paradoxes.

A number of objections have been posed to the pessimistic meta-induction, most pointing to the progress of science and the greater reliability of theories to predict results. However, there is far less appreciable progress in the history of solutions to paradoxes. In fact, some of the same solutions posited by the ancient philosophers are still posited today. Moreover, there is nothing like the consensus of acceptance that we see for scientific theories in solutions to philosophical paradoxes.

However, at least one of the objections may be applicable. Ronald Giere has insisted that philosophy of science is normative and not factual and that therefore the history of science cannot be relevant to the philosophy of science. Giere also claims that philosophers of science must criticize past theories and that in order to do so, they must have independent, nonhistorical grounds for this critique (Laudan 1977, 158–159). Applied to the present issue, a parallel argument can be made for the relevance of the history of philosophical paradoxes to their solutions. Why should this sad history have any claim upon the value of the solutions that are presently in the offing? Why should past failures take away any plausibility from present solutions? Such an objection points to a further question about the role of inductive evidence in philosophical methodology. Yet such an argument can be accepted without much force to the present discussion because, in addition to the conceptual arguments given earlier, an inductive argument merely adds support to what was previously argued.

The present section traces the history of philosophical paradoxes from the ancient Greeks to recent analytic philosophers. Not surprisingly, this history runs parallel to the history of logic and mathematics, with certain golden ages for philosophical paradoxes that coincide with times of major innovations in logic. We begin with an account of the origins of paradox. Zeno of Elea, founder of dialectic and creator of paradoxes of space and motion, is often credited with being the first philosopher to create a paradox. Yet long before he created his paradoxes, a method used by the ancient mathematicians provided the foundation on which paradoxes emerged in Greece. Both Zeno and later Eubulides, who is credited with producing the liar paradox, cite Parmenides's work as important to their development, and both have used the paradoxes in attempts to show that the doctrines of Parmenides are no more counterintuitive than alternative doctrines.

Another golden era for paradox was the Middle Ages. The philosophers of this age had a seemingly endless passion for *insolubilia*, the paradoxes of material and strict implication, and, more rarely, paradoxes involving sets.[2] In addition, the philosophers of the Middle Ages did something that there is no evidence that earlier philosophers of paradox did: they presented competing solutions to the paradoxes and evaluated the solutions. As you'll see in section 3.3.2, these attempts at solutions were ultimately fruitless, though quite interesting.

Although the Renaissance may have been a time of rebirth in other disciplines, the time was a dark age for logic and paradox, and I won't spend much time discussing it. Numerous attacks on logic occurred during the Renaissance. Also, the medieval logical texts, including sections on *insolubilia*, were still being used without much improvement during the Renaissance and continued to be used until the late nineteenth century. And, with the dawn of the scientific revolution, certain paradoxes began to emerge regarding the philosophy of science. Yet despite the revolutions in science, mathematics, and inductive logic, there were not as many revolutionary developments in the study of paradox, making this time an intriguing and seemingly anomalous period in the history of paradox (Kneale and Kneale 1962, 298–230).

The late nineteenth century marked a turning point in mathematics and logic, with developments such as Georg Cantor's treatment of infinite numbers. As a result of these developments in mathematics and logic, there was a resurgence of paradoxes. The first paradoxes to emerge were those concerning sets, some reminiscent of paradoxes that arose in the Middle Ages. The set-theoretic paradoxes emerged in this period, and others soon followed. The early twentieth century brought with it renewed interest in the liar paradox, set-theoretic paradoxes, and paradoxes involving epistemology. The late twentieth and early twenty-first centuries have embraced the paradox as well. Developments in logic, such as degree theoretic logics, fuzzy logics, and the like all vie for prominence and purport to provide solutions to longstanding paradoxes such as the liar and the sorites paradoxes. None, however, has been universally adopted as a straightforward solution of types 1 through 4.[3]

3.2   From *Doxa* to *Paradoxa*: On the Origins of Paradox in Western Philosophy

They fashioned a tomb for you, o holy and high one
The Cretans, always liars, evil beasts, idle bellies!
But thou art not dead; Thou livest and abidest forever
—Epimenides (a Cretan), *Cretica*

The common wisdom on philosophical paradoxes is that they first appeared with the ancient Greek philosopher Zeno of Elea (who reached his prime around 500 BCE) and his famous arguments on space, motion, and plurality. Although there is surely some truth to this view, the fuller picture is that paradoxes arise in Western philosophy thanks to forces from both within and outside what we now consider to be philosophical terrain. Long before Zeno gave the Achilles and the tortoise, arrow, racetrack, stadium, and other arguments, the method of indirect proof that provides the structure for paradoxes was introduced into ancient mathematics. In addition, Xenophanes—the mentor of Zeno's own mentor, Parmenides—used an argument structure similar to Zeno's in his critique of the theological views given by Homer and other writers. Careful study of the origins of paradox reveals that not only were there precursors to and influences on Zeno's arguments but also that the ancients had, in some ways, more successful approaches to paradox than contemporary philosophers who emphasize the production of logical systems on which paradoxes do not arise.

The first proponents of what are now taken to be philosophical paradoxes had a somewhat different approach to their arguments. Zeno's arguments for example, were not intended as paradoxes, at least in any of the senses in which the term "paradox" is presently understood. Two standard definitions, Sainsbury's (2009) and Rescher's (2001), assume that paradoxes take the form of a demonstrative proof. For Sainsbury, a paradox is an unacceptable conclusion derived from seemingly true premises using seemingly good reasoning. And for Rescher, a paradox is an argument with seemingly true premises and seemingly good reasoning leading to an obviously false or contradictory conclusion. Zeno, on the other hand, gives an indirect proof in which an assumption is made and then a contradiction is derived, thereby showing the assumption to be false.

Because of the strongly negative intuitive force of their demonstrations, the earliest paradoxes were often associated with the dialectical method, a type of reasoning in which a statement is proven by assuming its opposite and deriving an unacceptable consequence. Zeno of Elea often used the dialectical method. In fact, Aristotle claims that Zeno introduced the dialectical method into philosophy (Kneale and Kneale 1962, 7).

The ancient term that *dialectic* is derived from was used as the first technical term to refer to *logic* (Kneale and Kneale 1962). The ancient Greek word that *logic* derives from was not used to refer to the study of reasoning until the third century AD. The earliest, prelogical meaning of *dialectic* was *to discuss*. Later, *dialectic* acquired a series of closely related technical meanings that all involved the method of refutation. In one sense, the *method of dialectic* was used to mean the use of what was later called *modus tollens*, the rule of inference that asserts that *If P, then Q* and *Not Q* imply *Not P*. More specific uses included the methods of *reductio ad impossibile*, the deriving of a contradiction from an assumed premise and *reductio ad absurdum*, the deriving of an absurd consequence from an assumed premise. In all methods, an unacceptable consequence shows that the denial of a proposition is true. Unlike in its counterpart, demonstrative reasoning (in which the premises are known to be true and a true conclusion derived from them), in dialectical reasoning, a premise is assumed and if an unacceptable consequence is derived from it, then its denial is proven.

Zeno used the dialectical method to critique the assumptions of those who attacked his mentor Parmenides's view that "what is, is one." In Plato's dialogue *Parmenides*, Zeno describes his strategy as using the same method as used by Parmenides's critics in order to show that even more ridiculous consequences would follow for the critics' assumption that there *is* a plurality of things (Plato 2005 922). Consider, for example, any object that we would normally consider to be composed of a plurality of parts, such as the following line:

Box 21

A divided line

A line is thought to be composed of an infinite number of points. But, if this is so, what length can each point have? If each point has some extremely small but finite length, then the line would have to be infinitely long, because the line is composed of an infinite number of points. However, if each point has no length, then the line too should have no length because each part has a length of zero. Thus, it seems to follow that what we normally think about pluralities such as lines leads us to conclude either of two equally absurd things: that lines are infinitely long or that they have no length at all.

This type of reasoning applies to size, as well—what Zeno calls *magnitude*. In his commentary, Simplicius describes Zeno as arguing along the following lines:

> Having first shown that "if what is had not magnitude, it would not exist at all," he proceeds: "But, if it is, then each one must necessarily have some magnitude and thickness and must be at a certain distance from another. And the same reasoning holds good of the one beyond: for it also will have magnitude and there will be a successor to it. It is the same to say this once and to say it always: for no such part will be the last not out of relation to another. So, if there is a plurality, they must be both small and large. So small as to have no magnitude, so large as to be infinite. (Lee 1967, 21)

Although Simplicius is saying that the conclusion Zeno draws is that pluralities must be *both* infinitely large *and* not have a size at all, the conclusion to be drawn from this reasoning is slightly different. Zeno takes the assumption that there is a plurality and derives not a contradiction but an absurdity, namely, that there must be *either* an infinitely large collection of things *or* have no size at all. If there is a multiplicity of things, then each thing will be composed of other, smaller things, and so on, ad infinitum. Now if each of this infinite collection of things has no magnitude, then it will be nothing, and hence the plurality of things will have no magnitude. Yet, if each of the plurality has some magnitude, because there are infinitely many parts to the plurality, it must be infinitely large. Thus, Zeno concludes, there is not a plurality of things. What is, is one. Taking the assumption that there is plurality, Zeno derives the consequence that it would have to be infinitely large or else of no magnitude. Because both of these options are absurd, he concludes that there is no such plurality.

Zeno applied his dialectical method to motion as well. In Achilles and the tortoise, Zeno starts with the ordinary notion of motion and then shows how contradiction results from it. Even though Achilles is faster than the tortoise, he can never catch up to it in a race. If the tortoise starts out a small distance ahead of Achilles, then Achilles must get from his starting point to the point from which the tortoise started. While he is doing this, the tortoise has moved a small distance from its starting point. Achilles must then get to this point. But in the time he does this, the tortoise has moved again. And so on. Because the tortoise is constantly moving, by the time Achilles reaches the point the tortoise was previously, the tortoise has moved, however slowly it may have done so. Thus, Achilles can never catch the tortoise.

In describing this argument, commentators such as Aristotle and Simplicius see the connection between the Achilles and the tortoise argument and another argument, the dichotomy. In the latter argument, the conclusion is that a person cannot get from point A to point B, because to do so the person would have to make an infinite number of "journeys." The line connecting A to B is infinitely divisible; hence the person who goes from A to B must pass through an infinite number of points. And because it is impossible to complete an infinite number of journeys, no one can get from A to B. Aristotle sees the connection between the two arguments as follows:

This is that the slowest runner will never be overtaken by the swiftest, since the pursuer must first reach the point from which the pursued started. This argument is essentially the same as that depending on dichotomy, but differs in that the successively given lengths are not divided into halves. The conclusion of the argument is that the slowest runner is not overtaken, but it proceeds on the same lines as the dichotomy argument (for in both, by dividing the distance in a given way, we conclude that the goal is not reached: only in the Achilles a dramatic effect is produced by saying that not even the swiftest will be successful in its pursuit of the slowest). (Aristotle, *Physics*, Z 9.239b)

In both paradoxes, the notion of infinite divisibility is used to draw the conclusion that motion is impossible. Because the tortoise is moving more slowly than Achilles, the distance between it and Achilles gets progressively smaller. But because the tortoise is constantly moving to some finite degree, it will always move a small amount past the point where it began. The difference between the tortoise and Achilles's positions gets progressively smaller but never reaches zero. Similarly, in the dichotomy, because the "journeys" that someone must travel to get from A to B is infinite, a person, it seems, can never complete all of the journeys.

In the paradox of the arrow, Zeno again assumes that something, such as an arrow, moves through space. He then exposes a hidden inconsistency with this assumption. Something is at rest, according to Zeno, if it occupies the space equal to itself. Assume that an arrow is moving through space. At any instant in time, the arrow will occupy the space equal to itself. So, at any given instant, the object will be at rest. And because the time it takes the arrow to go through space is composed of such instants, the arrow will always be at rest. Because space is made up of a series of points, the arrow will pass through these points in going from A to B. But at each of these points, the arrow will occupy the space equal to itself. At every point, then, it will be at rest.

The dialectical method is also used in Zeno's less known and less successful paradox of the Stadium. In the stadium, Zeno attempts to show that where there are three rows of objects, the first being stationary and the other two moving at equal velocities in opposite directions, the time it takes for one of the moving rows to pass the other is both double and half. Consider rows A, B, and C and the ends of the "stadium" D and E:

Box 22

```
Zeno's stadium


                    A A A A
    D                   B B B B →              E
                  ←C C C C
```

Row A is stationary and rows B and C are moving at equal velocity in opposite directions. Row B begins at the midpoint of Row A and moves toward E. Row C also begins at the midpoint of A and moves toward D. As they move past each other, the first C will pass all four Bs in the same time it takes for the first B to pass only two As. So, Zeno concludes that, even though B and C are supposed to be moving with equal velocity and crossing equal distances, C has passed more points than B has.

The weakness of this argument seems to be generally acknowledged by Zeno's early commentators. In *Physics*, Aristotle says, "The fallacy lies in assuming that a body takes an equal time to pass with equal velocity a body that is in motion and a body of equal size at rest" (9.239 b 33). Similarly, Simplicius claims, "The fallacy lies in assuming without qualification that movements past bodies of equal size take an equal time, without taking into account the further fact that of the equal bodies some are moving in the opposite direction and some are stationary" (Lee 1967, 61). However, although Zeno's stadium argument is far less interesting than his other arguments, the line of reasoning he uses again illustrates that he is primarily concerned with taking an assumption—in this case, about motion—and showing how contradiction results.

The dialectical method is very powerfully applied in many of Zeno's arguments, and Xenophanes used a similar method earlier in his critique of Homer's views about the nature of the gods. Lee (1997), for example, gives Theophrastus's interpretation of Xenophanes's critique on the idea of a multiplicity of gods: "It is natural that god should be one, for if there were two or more, he would not be the most powerful and most excellent of all. . . . If, then, there were several beings, some stronger, some weaker, they would not be gods; for it is not the nature of god to be ruled. Nor would they have the nature of god if they were equal, for god ought to be the most powerful" (36). In the latter part of the quote, Xenophanes is described as claiming that if there is more than one god, then there would be at least one god that is less powerful than another. And because it is part of the nature of a god to be the most powerful being, there cannot be more than one god. This argument uses modus tollens in arguing that if polytheism is correct, then a false consequence follows, and concluding that polytheism is incorrect.

Theophrastus further writes:

> And [Xenophanes] shows that god must have been without beginning, since whatever comes into being must come either from what is like it or from what is unlike it; but, he says, it is no more natural to think that like should give birth to like, than that like should be born from like; but if it had sprung from what is unlike it, then being would have sprung from non-being. . . . For even if the stronger were to come from the weaker, the greater from the less, or the better from the worse, or on the other hand the worse from the better, still being could not come from not-being, since this is impossible. Accordingly, god is eternal. (Lee 1967, 36)

Here Xenophanes is arguing that the god must be eternal (without beginning). If it were the case that a god had a beginning, then certain implausible consequences would follow. One is that the like must be born of the like, and Xenophanes thinks that this cannot happen in the case of the god, perhaps because the god is being. Or else the like must come from the unlike. Because god, for Xenophanes, was being, that would mean coming into existence from nonbeing. Neither option is good, according to Xenophanes. Thus, the god is eternal, having no beginning or end. If you consider Xenophanes to be a philosopher and not merely a poet, the introduction of dialectic into philosophy comes from him or someone who lived before him.

In his famous poem, Parmenides—Xenophanes's student and the mentor of Zeno—uses a similar ploy to argue that Being is eternal. He writes:

> There is a solitary word still left to say of a way:
> "exists"; very many signs are on this road: that Being
> is ungenerated and imperishable, whole, unique,
> immovable, and complete. It was not once nor will it
> be, since it is now altogether, one, continuous. For,
> what origin could you search out for it? How and
> whence did it grow? Not from non-Being shall I allow
> you to say or to think, for it is not possible to say or
> to think that it is not. What need would have made
> it grow, beginning, from non-Being, later or sooner?

Thus it is necessary either to exist all in all or not at all. (Tarán 1965, Fragment VIII)

As in Xenophanes's argument for a timeless god, Parmenides argues that Being is timeless because absurdity follows from the idea that being is in time. Thus, the dialectical method of argumentation was used by both Zeno's mentor Parmenides and Parmenides's mentor, Xenophanes. It is plausible to suppose that the first Western paradoxes, which use a similar dialectical method, were based in part on these earlier arguments.

Another source of inspiration for Zeno was probably the Pythagoreans and their use of dialectical methods of proof in mathematics. An example of such a proof is that the square root of 2 is irrational. The Pythagoreans argued along the following lines: assume that the square root of 2 is rational. That is, assume that there are two mutually prime integers, n and m, such that n/m = the square root of 2. Put another way, $n^2 = 2m^2$. If this is so, then because a square number cannot have any prime factor that is not also a factor of the number of which it is the square, n^2 and n must be even. But according to our initial assumption, n and m are mutually prime, so if n is even, then m must be odd. Assuming that $n = 2k$, we get $2m^2 = 4k^2$ or $m^2 = 2k^2$; then, by repeating the same reasoning, we can show that m is even. Thus, n must be both odd and even. So in assuming that the square root of 2 is rational, we have derived a contradiction. Thus, the square root of 2 is irrational.

As this proof illustrates, the Pythagoreans were already using a method very similar to the one that Zeno used in his proofs. The proof begins with the assumption that the square root of 2 is rational and then derives a contradiction. Zeno, who was engaged in a long intellectual battle with the Pythagoreans, used their own methods to show that Pythagorean ideas about space were flawed. In Plato's *Parmenides*, for example, Zeno explains the purpose of his now-lost book to a young Socrates:

> The book is in fact a sort of defense of Parmenides'
> argument against those who try to make fun of it
> by showing that his supposition, that there is a one,
> leads to many absurdities and contradictions. This
> book, then, is a retort against those who assert a
> plurality. It pays them back in the same coin with
> something to spare, and aims at showing that, on
> a thorough examination, their own supposition
> that there is a plurality leads to even more absurd
> consequences than the hypothesis of the one. (Plato
> 2005, 128D)

Although it is unclear to whom Zeno was referring in this selection, it is quite plausible that he was referring to the Pythagoreans. Because Parmenides was associated with a Pythagorean, Ameinias, who was the son of Diochaitis and uses a dialectical method similar to the Pythagoreans', there should have been some kind of connection. Zeno, having already encountered Xenophanes's and Parmenides's critical methods, as well as the work of the Pythagoreans, and being aware that a main objection to Parmenides's view was that it was counterintuitive, turns the method of indirect proof against the Pythagorean view that there is a plurality. The first paradoxes, in the Western tradition, then, were attempts to show that seemingly commonsensical ideas about space, motion, and plurality are not so commonsensical, using the indirect method of proof used by the very same philosophers that criticized Parmenides's view as being counterintuitive.

The strongly counterintuitive view that change is an illusion was the subject of much ridicule by other philosophical schools. It is understandable, then, why Zeno would propound arguments to the effect that the critics of Parmenides had views that led to equally counterintuitive consequences. The intuitiveness of various positions, then, was an influential factor in the development of philosophical paradoxes. Because paradoxes are arguments with *seemingly* true premises and *obviously* false or contradictory conclusions, they play on our intuitions. Paradoxes invite us to confront our strong intuitions about commonsense notions such as truth, baldness, motion, and the like. Thus, it is plausible to think that the intent of giving the first paradoxes was to show that the "seemingly" commonsensical views about motion and space led to strongly counterintuitive conclusions. Zeno showed that sometimes common sense—*eudoxa* in the Ancient Greek— leads to paradox—*paradoxa*, literally *against* or *beyond* the common *opinion* or *expectation*.

Intellectual battles, theological arguments, ancient mathematics, and Zeno himself are all part of the story of the origins of paradox in Western philosophy. In defending the view of his mentor, Parmenides, against charges of counterintuitive conclusions, Zeno used the dialectical method to derive even more counterintuitive conclusions for the denial of Parmenides's view that "what is, is one."

3.3 Alternative Conceptions of Solutions from A(ristotle) to Z(eno) and Beyond

What we have come to call *paradoxes* were, for Zeno, arguments that proved that the assumptions of Parmenides's critics led to as many absurd conclusions as the counterintuitive Parmenidean view that change is an illusion. Thus, the origin of solutions to paradoxes does not begin with Zeno. If we look to Eubulides, who is sometimes credited with creating the liar paradox, we again find that the paradox was not created with the intention of being solved but rather as a critique of a commonly held assumption—in

It is plausible to think that the intent of giving the first paradoxes was to show that the "seemingly" common-sensical views about motion and space led to strongly counter-intuitive conclusions.

this case, the assumption that the world is composed of a plurality of things (Kneale and Kneale 1962, 15–16).

Most likely, we have Aristotle to thank for the first standard solutions to paradoxes. Aristotle not only presented a method of critiquing arguments that involved pointing to a false premise in an argument, but he also maintained that the air of seeming truth to the false part must be explained in the "solution" to what he called "refutations." In addition, Aristotle had much to say about the paradoxes that were discussed at the time, including Zeno's paradoxes and the liar paradox. Aristotle's solutions and those of later philosophers were unsuccessful for many of the same reasons. A broad look at the history of solutions to philosophical paradox reveals the same or similar failed solutions repeated throughout the ages with various paradoxes.

One common way for a solution to fail, for example, is for the solution to be unable to sidestep the paradox if the paradox is put in slightly different terms (e.g., denying bivalence for the liar, but not excluded middle). The patterns of failure are useful in that they provide the evidence needed for the pessimistic meta-induction argument given earlier. In addition, knowing this history of solutions will help future solvers of paradoxes avoid, if possible, some of the more common ways in which solutions to paradoxes fail.

3.3.1 Aristotle and the Origins of Solutions to Paradoxes

It is impossible in a discussion to bring in the actual things discussed: we use their names as symbols instead of them; and therefore we suppose that what follows in the names, follows in the things as well, just as people who calculate suppose in regard to their counters. But the two cases (names and things) are not alike. For names are finite and so is the sum-total of formulae, while things are infinite in number. Inevitably, then, the same formulae, and a single name, have a number of meanings. Accordingly just as, in counting, those who are not clever in manipulating their counters are taken in by the experts, in the same way in arguments too those who are not well acquainted with the force of names misreason both in their own discussions and when they listen to others. For this reason, then, and for others to be mentioned later, there exists both reasoning and refutation that is apparent but not real.

—Aristotle, *Sophistical Refutations*, book I, chapter i

The main discussions of philosophical paradoxes in Aristotle's surviving work occur in *Sophistical Refutations* and *Physics*. In *Sophistical Refutations*, he seems to use the term "paradox" somewhat loosely, sometimes to mean an unacceptable consequence and sometimes as fallacious arguments. In addition, his treatment of the liar paradox and Zeno's paradoxes shows that he thought of them as fallacious arguments and hence did not think of fallacious arguments and paradoxes as occupying two distinct types of argument. Leading an opponent to utter a paradox is listed by Aristotle as one of the methods used by the Sophists to seem wise. He then gives instructions to the competitive speaker for getting one's opponent to utter a statement that can lead to paradox. For example, he maintains:

> Again, to elicit a paradox you should know to what school the person who is discussing with you belongs, and then question him on some pronouncement of that school which most people regard as paradoxical; for every school has some tenet of this kind. An elementary rule in this connection is to have a ready-made collection of theses of the different schools among your propositions. The proper solution is to make it clear that the paradox does not result because of the argument. (*Sophistical Refutations*, 172b)

It is unclear in this passage whether Aristotle means by "paradox" anything like we presently mean, and by "solution" he seems to mean a way of showing that the paradox does not apply to the present issue.

Sophistical Refutations is Aristotle's main work on logical errors and the ways in which to resolve them. For Aristotle, there are four types of syllogisms: (1) demonstrative, which proceeds from true and primary premises, (2) dialectical, which proceeds from common beliefs, (3) false "eristic" reasoning, which falsely simulates dialectical, and something called *endoxic*, reasoning, and (4) false reasoning, which simulates demonstrative reasoning. These arise from false scientific premises. The main target of Aristotle's discussion is the use of eristic reasoning by the Sophists, and he wishes to give solutions to these. A resolution to an argument that falsely simulates dialectical reasoning requires two things. First, the resolution must explain why the argument falsely mirrors the correct form of reasoning. And second, it must explain why the argument appeared convincing (*Sophistical Refutations*, 3–4).

Although Aristotle did not focus on philosophical paradoxes alone when giving guidelines for resolutions to the sophistical arguments, he uses his own guidelines in his treatment of Zeno's paradox and in his treatment of the liar paradox. For Aristotle, the liar paradox is an example of the fallacy *secundum quid et simpliciter*, that is, confusing things in a certain respect (*secundum quid*) with things absolutely (*simpliciter*). In *Sophistical Refutations*, Aristotle treats the liar paradox as analogous to a lesser-known paradox, the perjurer, in which someone vows to break his own oath:

Nor if a man keeps his oath in this particular instance
or in this particular respect, is he bound also to be a
keeper of oaths absolutely, but he who swears that
he will break his oath, and then breaks it, keeps this
particular oath only; he is not a keeper of his oath;
nor is the disobedient man "obedient," though he
obey this one particular command. This argument
is similar, also, as regards the problem whether the
same man can at the same time say what is both false
and true: but it appears to be a troublesome question
because it is not easy to see in which of the two
connections the word "absolutely" is to be rendered—
with "true" or with "false." There is, however, nothing
to prevent it from being false absolutely, though true
in some particular respect or relation, i.e., being true
in some things, though not true absolutely. (Spade
1988, 30)

For Aristotle, the perjurer keeps his oath (to break his
oath) in breaking some other oath at a later time. Absolutely speaking, the man is a perjurer, but not relative to
his oath to break the oath, "I shall break my oath." Aristotle
then says that the liar example is of the same sort, apparently meaning that the liar sentence is not true absolutely
but is true in some particular respect. To clarify his point,
Aristotle next draws a parallel between the liar and other
fallacious arguments:

Likewise also in cases of some particular relation and place and time. For all arguments of the following kind depend upon this. "Is health, or wealth, a good thing?" "Yes." "But to the fool who does not use it aright it is not a good thing: therefore it is both good and not good." "Is health, or political power, a good thing?" "Yes." "But sometimes it is not particularly good: therefore the same thing is both good and not good to the same man." (*Sophistical Refutations*, book I, chapter xxv)

So although a claim may be true *in general*, in particular it may not be. For the sentence "I am a liar," Aristotle holds that it may be true in general but not relative to the particular utterance made by the person. This solution, however, applies only to cases in which it is possible to separate out an absolute and a particular context. If, for example, I say, "I am lying right now," it seems hard to claim that such a sentence, which refers to a particular utterance, could be true absolutely, but false in the particular. The sentence refers, particularly, to itself and hence cannot be claimed true in general.

Although Aristotle's treatment of the liar paradox is sketchy at best, his treatment of Zeno's paradoxes is detailed and complete, and he discusses multiple paradoxes of Zeno. In *Physics*, Aristotle claims that with respect to the arrow, "Zeno's reasoning, however, is fallacious, when he says that if everything when it occupies an equal space is at rest, and if that which is in locomotion is always occupying such a space at any moment, the flying arrow is therefore motionless. This is false, for time is not composed of indivisible moments any more than any other magnitude is composed of indivisibles" (*Physics*, book VI, chapter ix). Here, Aristotle is giving an Odd-Guy-Out solution to Zeno's paradox of the arrow, which denies that the arrow is never moving because, at any point, it is occupying the space equal to itself, and no other. The Odd-Guy-Out here, for Aristotle, is the assumption that time and space are composed of indivisibles. Because we cannot divide time into indivisible instants, the arrow must move through some duration. Once we get rid of this assumption, then there is no problem with assuming that the arrow is moving from one physical space to another.

Aristotle lodges another criticism of an assumption made by many of Zeno's paradoxes, namely the assumption that something cannot travel past an infinite number of things in a finite time. Aristotle charges that

> Zeno's argument makes a false assumption in asserting that it is impossible for a thing to pass over or severally to come in contact with infinite things in a finite time. For there are two senses in which length

and time and generally anything continuous are called "infinite": they are called so either in respect of divisibility or in respect of their extremities. So while a thing in a finite time cannot come in contact with things quantitatively infinite, it can come in contact with things infinite in respect of divisibility: for in this sense the time itself is also infinite: and so we find that the time occupied by the passage over the infinite is not a finite but an infinite time, and the contact with the infinites is made by means of moments not finite but infinite in number. (*Physics*, book VI, chapter ii)

As in the earlier solution to the arrow, Aristotle here gives an Odd-Guy-Out solution to Zeno's paradoxes of motion, claiming that Zeno conflates infinity as a quantitative notion with infinity as a notion concerned with divisibility. Because these two things cannot be interchanged, Zeno is not licensed in assuming that because space is infinitely divisible, it would take an infinite amount of time to get from any point to another.

It is hard to overstate Aristotle's influence on later logicians and would-be solvers of paradoxes, which becomes most apparent, as you'll soon see, in the solutions of the philosophers and logicians of the Middle Ages.

3.3.2   Insolubilia in the Middle Ages

As for insolubles, you should know it is not because they
can in no way be solved that some sophisms are called
insolubles, but because they are solved *with difficulty*.

—William of Ockham, *Summa logicae* III-3, 46

Although Aristotle was the earliest source of standard
solutions to philosophical paradoxes, treatments of solutions to paradoxes reached a golden age in the late Middle
Ages, when "insolubilia" received widespread attention by
logicians. In the early Middle Ages, most mentions of the
liar paradox gave variations of Aristotle's solution, namely,
that the paradox involved the fallacy of *secundum quid et
simpliciter*. Later, though, new analyses of the paradox
emerged as a wide variation of formulations of the paradox.

The sheer number and variety of proposed solutions ri-
vals the ubiquity of solutions that are proffered nowadays.
One marked distinction between recent solutions and
those of the Middle Ages is that present solutions often
arise, as a response to some kind of crisis in our thought.
The solutions of the Middle Ages don't seem to consider
the paradoxes as presenting crises to established theories.
Also, philosophers in the Middle Ages tended to focus on
various versions of the liar paradox, and contemporary
philosophers focus on multiple paradoxes. Here is a sam-
pling of restriction theories, the Middle Ages Preemptive

Although Aristotle was the earliest source of standard solutions to philosophical paradoxes, treatments of solutions to paradoxes reached a golden age in the late Middle Ages, when "insolubilia" received widespread attention by logicians.

Strike of choice. These theories try to restrict self-reference, saying that in some or all cases, terms that appear in statements cannot refer to the statements themselves.

Transcasus: An Early Restriction Theory

The transcasus solution treats the liar sentence *I am lying* as meaning that what the speaker of the sentence said before is false, and if nothing came before this sentence, then it is false. Similarly, *This sentence is false* refers to the sentence that comes before it, and if no sentence in fact came before the sentence, then it is false. In treating the liar sentence this way, the proponent of this type of solution restricts the reference of the sentence to a previous one and denies a referent to it when there is no previous sentence. Such a restriction, though, seems an ad hoc response to the paradox.

Cassation

Archaic for "canceling," *cassation* is the name of a theory that holds that when one utters an insoluble like *I am lying now*, one isn't saying anything at all. In denying that the speaker of the liar sentence is saying something, the theory of cassation provides a Preemptive Strike solution to the liar paradox. The liar sentence is defective, according to this view. To explain why, and to lower our subjective probability that someone who utters the liar sentence is actually saying something, the proponents of this type of solution have given two types of explanations. The first, a simple argument from ordinary language, holds that the man on the street, the *rusticus* (Spade 2009), if confronted with someone uttering *What I am saying is false* would most likely respond *You aren't saying anything at all*. Such a solution doesn't seem to be grounded in anything but the ordinary person's suspicion of claims that are not completely straightforward.

Another way the proponents of cassation try to lower the subjective probability that the utterer of the liar sentence is saying something is by providing an explanation of what it is to *say something* and showing that the utterer of the liar sentence does not qualify. To *say something*, this line of argument goes, requires that the speaker mentally asserts what is said, and vocally asserts it, too. Although the speaker of the liar sentence meets both conditions, something about the way the speaker does this is not correct. What it is, though, remains a mystery. Vincent Spade, a scholar of insolubilia literature, has posited tentatively that this could be something like the fallacy of composition, in which someone can, for example, be gifted and a cellist, but not a gifted cellist, if in fact his or her gifts lie in other things. But he is rightly tentative about assuming that this was what the proponent of cassation meant. At any rate, the proponents of both transcasus and cassation point to some type of flaw in the sentence that leads to paradox; hence both present Preemptive Strike solutions to the liar paradox.

Bradwardine's Theory of Truth

The most influential medieval Preemptive Strike solution against the liar paradox, at least among its contemporaries, came from Thomas Bradwardine, who proposed a theory of truth which holds that propositions signify things by virtue of their constituent terms, and that a proposition signifies the contents of a that-clause, asserting that what it signifies is the case. Propositions are true if, and only if, they signify *only* what is the case, and false otherwise. The theory also holds that whatever follows from a proposition is also signified by it. A proposition is then true if and only if whatever follows from it is the case. On this account, then every proposition signifies that it itself is true. In the case of the liar sentence, then the liar sentence signifies that it itself is false. But, based on this theory, the proposition also signifies that it itself is true. But the proposition that the liar sentence expresses then can be true only when everything it signifies is the case. If the liar proposition is true, then it is false. But because the requirement is that everything that follows from a proposition must be the case for the proposition to be true, the argument doesn't go back around to show that the liar sentence is true. Put simply, because everything that follows from a proposition is signified by the proposition, and because propositions are true if and only if everything they signify is the case, the proposition expressed by *I am speaking falsely* must signify something that is not the case. It is thus false.

The paradox is then solved, because the liar sentence turns out to be false, and the reason for this is that in addition to signifying that it is false, it also signifies that it is true. And this is not the case.

One immediate question arises, though, about the theory's assumption that everything that follows from a proposition is signified by it, which strikes me as counterintuitive. On one hand, there is what a proposition signifies, and on the other, what follows from it. Lots of things follow from one proposition, so the account seems to imply a very bloated conception of what it means for a proposition to signify something.[4]

Heytesbury and the Burden of Proof

An interesting spin on the discussion of insolubles was given by William Heytesbury, who claimed that insolubles were paradoxical only in certain restricted contexts. Saying that Margaret is lying is a paradox only when Margaret is the one that is making this claim about herself. Heytesbury says that in the case in which Margaret is herself saying that she is lying, the proposition *Margaret is lying* must signify something in addition to what the words ordinarily mean. And—here is a unique strategy—he maintains that the burden of proof doesn't fall on him to present the additional signification. As Spade (2009) notes, "In short, Heytesbury's strategy is to say, "You tell me *exactly* what [Margaret's] statement signifies, and I'll tell you first of all whether the case you describe is possible, and if it is, I'll tell you whether [the] statement is true or false." To my ears, this sounds like a deflection, and apparently it did as well to thinkers of the time. Others provided the additional signification: namely, that it also signifies that it is true. Later thinkers, in other words, added a little bit of Bradwardine's theory to Heytesbury's.

Conclusion

From this brief look at a few of the many proposed treatments of the insolubles, a pattern starts to emerge. The solutions tend toward the preemptive strike strategy for solving paradoxes, though each presents a different way of explaining why the liar sentence either "says nothing" or is false. Though interesting, none of the proposed solutions presents a definitive solution to the paradox.

3.3.3 Kant's Resolutions and Their Antinomies

One of the most intriguing responses to paradox comes from the philosopher Immanuel Kant, who discusses a number of *antinomies* in detail in his *Critique of Pure Reason*. Antinomies are sometimes defined as *conflicts between two laws*. Although antinomies are usually not considered paradoxes per se, they do contain some of the essential features of paradoxes mentioned in the introduction to this book; namely, they involve conflicting claims that are both well-supported. Kant's conception of the antinomy most closely resembles the account of paradox which holds that paradoxes are sets of mutually inconsistent statements, each of which seems true. An antinomy, for Kant, is a set of two mutually inconsistent but rational results. The two mutually inconsistent claims (e.g., there is free will and there is no free will) are what Kant calls his *thesis* and *antithesis*, and each is the conclusion of a seemingly persuasive argument. So we have two mutually inconsistent claims, each of which is supported with persuasive evidence. Although they are often considered distinct from paradoxes, Kant's antinomies are therefore a variety of paradox, one in which two conflicting claims are each given strong arguments to support them.

In his *Critique*, Kant focuses on four main antinomies, presenting side-by-side arguments for opposite conclusions. For example, the first antinomy concerns space and time and whether they are limited. On one side of the section discussing the antinomy, Kant presents an argument that time had a beginning and that space has a limit. In other words, he presents an argument that there was a beginning to the "world" and that the "world" has a physical limit. On the other side of the antinomy, Kant presents an argument that space and time have no such limits. Both arguments take the form of indirect proofs, like the arguments that Zeno gave, in which the denial of what is to be proven is assumed and then a contradiction is drawn, thus proving that the denial of the point to be proven must be false. In other words, assume that whatever you want to prove, such as *p*, is not true. Then show that when we assume the denial of *p* (i.e., *not p*), a contradiction or obvious falsehood results. In showing this, we can thus conclude *p*. Both arguments in the first antinomy, Kant claims, are justified given our background assumptions. Table 6 contains rewordings of how they are presented.

The left side of the first antinomy may sound similar to Zeno and his paradoxes of space and motion and may now suggest an easy resolution via the claim that infinite divisibility does not entail an endless number of "parts." The right side of the equation may bring to mind the idea of a limit to a series, as well.

Kant, though, takes a different route in dealing with this first antinomy, one based on his view that metaphysical questions—such as questions about whether the world has a beginning in space and time, whether there is free will, and whether the whole world consists of indivisible atoms—cannot be given satisfactory answers. For Kant, these questions involve an attempt to illegitimately use "concepts of pure reason," those without any ties to sense experience. As Kant famously claimed (1969, 93; A52/B76), such concepts without intuitions [involving sense experience] are empty. We can never draw inferences about the totality of the world from our own limited experience, which is given through the senses. For Kant, to think about "the world" as something that can be understood this way

Table 6   Kant's first antinomy, simplified

- -

Proof that (i) the world is limited in time and (ii) space

(i) First, assume that there was no temporal beginning to the world. If this is so, then there must have been an infinity of moments that led up to the present. But, in an infinite series, it is impossible for the parts of the series to be completed in succession. So, it is impossible for an infinite series to have passed away prior to the present moment. So, it is impossible for the world to have had no beginning in time.

(ii) First, assume that the world is unlimited in terms of space. That is, assume that the world is an infinite whole, composed of an infinite number of aggregate parts. But to think of the world as a whole of infinite parts means to add the parts together to form the whole. But, given that the number of parts is infinite, this cannot be done. An aggregate of an infinite number of things cannot be conceived, because it would require an endless adding of the parts, and this cannot be done.

Proof that (i) the world is not limited in time and (ii) space

(i) First, assume that there was a temporal beginning to the world. If this is so, then there must have been a time before the world's beginning, in other words, an empty time. However, nothing could come to be or pass away in empty time, because otherwise it wouldn't be empty. So, the world could not have come into being from empty time. This only leaves actual time. So, the world must have a beginning in time.

(ii) First, assume the world is limited in terms of space. That is, assume the world has a spatial limit, after which is empty space. But the world cannot be related to empty space. Because empty space is, by definition, empty, there is no object to which the world can be related in empty space. There is no object to which the limit corresponds. So, there can be no spatial limit to the world.

is to commit a serious mistake—namely, the mistake of thinking of the world as a "thing in itself" that can be understood by our own limited resources.

As with all his antinomies, the left-hand side illustrates our rational capacity to think beyond our limited experience. We start with our notion of infinity and conclude that there could be no infinite series of moments before the present and that there could be no unlimited space. The right-hand side pulls us back to the realm of experience. Both sides assume that there is a world and that this world is knowable to us. Both sides also assume that there is either a spatial/temporal limit to the world, or there is none. In the assumption that there is a world that can be understood in its totality, independent of our own limited experience, both arguments are flawed. Conceived as a paradox, the contradictory conclusion claiming that the world is both limited and unlimited with respect to space and time is the result of a faulty assumption: the assumption that the world, as a thing in itself, is knowable. Kant's solution to this antinomy, then, is closest to the Odd-Guy-Out in rejecting an assumption made by the paradox.

Kant's second antinomy is similar to the first in that it focuses, again, on the notion of a "world" that is to be known independent of our sense experience. Both antinomies get an Odd-Guy-Out solution. For the second antinomy, the issue is whether the world is composed of simple irreducible entities (substances) or whether the world can be divided infinitely. On the left-hand side of the antinomy, Kant presents a proof that the world is composed of simple parts, and on the right-hand side, he presents a proof that nothing is composed of simple parts (see table 7).

Table 7   Kant's second antinomy, simplified

Proof that every composite substance is composed of simple parts (and hence not infinitely divisible)	Proof that nothing is composed of simple parts (and that everything is infinitely divisible)
Proof: (1) Assume composite substances are not made up of simple parts. That is, assume that they are infinitely divisible. (2) If we take away all idea of composition from that of an infinitely divisible entity, there would be nothing left. And no basic substance, either. (3) So, either infinitely divisible entities are not made out of any simple substances, or there must remain something which exists, independently of the composition, namely, a simple substance. (4) But a composite substance must be made out of some substance. Otherwise, it would not be composed of anything. (5) Therefore, there must be simple substances out of which composite substances are formed.	Proof: (1) Assume that a composite thing is made up of simple parts. (2) Every part of this composite thing occupies a spatial location. (3) If something occupies space, then it is a composite entity. (4) Therefore, every part of a composite substance is itself composite.

For Kant, both sides of this antinomy rely on the same faulty assumption made by the proofs in the first antinomy, namely that the world as a whole can be understood independently of our intuition (i.e., sense experience). Both sides, then, are mistaken. Although I have characterized Kant as giving Odd-Guy-Out solutions to these antinomies, his approach doesn't completely merit this categorization, given that he acknowledges that it is part of the demands of reason to seek out and answer questions about mind-independent reality. So although both antinomies are the result of trying to go beyond the limits of our reason, it is nevertheless inevitable that reason will attempt to overreach its limits. In this sense, such antinomies are unavoidable. This result suggests that Kant's solutions have Facing-the-Music elements as well.

In the next two antinomies, Kant's strategy shifts from an Odd-Guy-Out/Facing-the-Music approach to something most resembling an It's-All-Good approach. Although both sides of each of the following two antinomies look as if they result in contradiction, when looked at in greater depth, the contradictions vanish. The third antinomy concerns free will and determinism, though the arguments center on the idea of causality and whether there can be anything that stands outside of the natural chain of events and has *absolute spontaneity* (table 8).

The left-hand side of the antinomy holds that the very idea of causality is itself something that assumes that there

Table 8 Kant's third antinomy, simplified

There is freedom of the will.	There is no freedom of the will.
First, assume that there is no freedom of the will, that is, that there is no causality other than that determined by the laws of nature. If this is so, then every event that occurs can be traced back to some event that is its cause. However, if we do this repeatedly, there will be an infinite regress of causes. If this is so, then there is no absolute causality, only relative causality. But, the law of nature states, "nothing takes place without a cause *sufficiently* determined *a priori*" (A446/B474; italics in original). So, in assuming that no causality takes place independently of the laws of nature, we have derived a contradiction, namely, that there is no absolute causality. Therefore, there must be at least one form of causality that stands outside the laws of nature. That is, something that has absolute spontaneity, "whereby a series of appearances, which proceeds in accordance with laws of nature, begins of itself. This is transcendental freedom" (A446/B474).	First, assume that there is freedom of the will. In other words, assume that there is a causality of actions that is not determined by the laws of nature, but instead absolutely determines itself. This causality that brings about other events is itself an event and violates a law of nature that assumes that every event has a preceding cause. It also stands outside sense-experience and is what Kant calls "an empty thought-entity" (A446/B474). "If freedom were determined in accordance with laws, it would not be freedom; it would simply be nature under another name" (A446/B474).

is something that stands outside it, an absolute cause that is sufficient to begin the chain of causality a priori. The right-hand side, on the other hand, assumes that there is such a causality, and shows that this, too, contradicts a law of nature: that events have causes and that there is an order to nature which makes it comprehensible to us, through our observation of it. Both of these two proofs are compatible, for Kant, as long as we give up the assumption that the world of appearances and our sense experience of the world around us are "things in themselves." If we give up this assumption, then we can hold that we are *both* required by reason to posit transcendental freedom (the left-hand side of the antinomy) *and* required by sense experience of the world to posit that all appearances conform to the laws of causality (table 9).

In each of the previous two antinomies, Kant argues that both sides of the antinomies are, in some sense, good arguments. Yet he claims that what looked like contradictory conclusions were really compatible statements. Thus, his approach to these last two antinomies most closely resembles an It's-All-Good approach.

In the case of the fourth antinomy, if we give up the idea that appearances are themselves "things in themselves," each side of the antinomy can peacefully coexist with the other. Reason, on the left, necessitates the idea of a necessary being, while appearances—the world of sense experience—prove that there can be no such being.

Table 9   Kant's fourth antinomy, simplified

An absolutely necessary being (i.e., God) exists	An absolutely necessary being (i.e., God) does not exist, either (i) in this world or (ii) as a cause of this world.
The sensible world changes. This is obvious when we consider that without change we couldn't even have the concept of time. Each change that occurs in the sensible world is preceded by earlier changes that make the present change necessary. But, conceived in general, all change then must be brought about by something that is absolutely neces-sary. As Kant wrote, "Alteration thus existing as a consequence of the absolutely necessary, the existence of something absolutely necessary must be granted" (452/B480). So there must be an absolutely necessary being. In addition, this necessary being must exist in the sensible world. Otherwise, how would the changes start? This necessary being must therefore, as Kant says, "belong to time and so to appearance" (454/B482). So, this necessary being must exist, temporally, in the world.	(i) Concerning a necessary being's existence in the world, assume that there is such an absolutely necessary being. If this is so, then either there is a beginning in the series of alterations that happen in time that is absolutely necessary and without a cause, or else there is no beginning to the series of alterations that happen in time. But the first option is no good, because it conflicts with the law that all appearances have to be predetermined in time. And the second is no good either, because it contradicts itself in assuming that there is a series that although necessary, has no member that is absolutely necessary. (ii) As for the existence of an absolutely necessary being outside of the world which causes everything to happen within it. If we assume that there is such a being, then this cause must begin all the alterations that are to happen in the sensible world.

The "resolution" to both antinomies lies, for Kant, in the distinction between the world as it appears to us: the phenomenal world, on the one hand, and the world beyond our sensible experience, as "a thing in itself," independent of us, on the other hand, or what Kant calls the *noumenal* world. Thus, while presenting us with an interesting variation on the paradox—the antinomy—Kant uses some standard solution-types for dealing with these paradoxes.

3.3.4 Later Solutions to Paradoxes

To give you a sense of the ubiquity of using logical systems to provide solutions to paradoxes in contemporary philosophy, permit me to recount a little story. When I was at a conference in Beijing a few years ago, I attended a number of sessions in which different logical systems were outlined. These different systems included degree-theories, supervaluationism, fuzzy logics, paraconsistent logic, logics with gaps, and so on. At the end of each session, the presenter would explain how his or her preferred logical system dealt with important paradoxes such as the liar paradox. Walking to lunch with a friend after one such presentation, I asked him what he thought about the conference. His response was that it was like going to a local fair, except that instead of hearing things such as "Here is my cow; she can sing," we hear things like "Here is my logic;

here are the paradoxes it solves." His response has stuck with me because of the variety of new logics that are on the market today. By introducing this new, "better" way of thinking about truth, falsity, and entailment, the proponent of the new system attempts to show how, under this system, the paradox does not arise. I have since begun calling these approaches, which fall into each solution-type in the previously described taxonomy, the Here-Is-My-Cow-She-Can-Sing approaches in honor of my friend.

I've briefly discussed most of these logics and their solutions to a particular paradox in the previous section, but let's take a look at them as a group. One of the things that has struck me as intriguing about contemporary logical systems is that despite their questionable utility for solving the deepest philosophical paradoxes, they are exceedingly useful in other domains. Although many of the paradoxes that inspired the creation of the various contemporary logics that are in the offing today still remain without definitive solutions, many practical uses for these logics make them "successful," at least in terms of the applications to extraphilosophical terrain. Table 10 contains a brief list of these uses. This list suggests a different way for thinking about the role of solutions and paradoxes. Paradoxes might not be problems that need to be quickly done away with but might rather serve as an impetus for revising folk concepts into more precise and useful ones.

Table 10 Contemporary systems and their uses

Logic	Sample uses
Three-valued logic	Used in SQL database language
Fuzzy and degree-theoretic logics	Used in fuzzy programming for air conditioners, handwriting recognition programs, traffic lights, etc.
Set theories	Used in studying the foundations of mathematics, and basis for molecular set theory
Supervaluationism	Helps in mapping vaguely defined objects like rivers
Bayesianism	Used in analyzing scientific evidence
Decision theory	Used in risk analysis, determining the expected monetary value (EMV) of a particular business decision
Game theory	Used to analyze human behavior, including economic behavior, and used in evolutionary theory

Solutions and paradoxes emerge in times of mathematical and scientific progress and are often the impetus to progress.

3.3.5 Conclusion to the Survey of Solutions

Though this glance through the history of solutions and paradoxes must necessarily be incomplete, it does suggest that certain conclusions can be reasonably drawn. First, nothing like consensus has ever been achieved for solutions to the most troubling paradoxes. Second, solutions and paradoxes emerge in times of mathematical and scientific progress and are often the impetus to progress. Although the deepest philosophical paradoxes remain unyielding to the many solutions given to them, the solutions themselves have been interesting and useful in their own right.

3.4 New Sciences, New Paradoxes

Paradoxes involve strong intuitions about the truth of claims that are in apparent conflict. They expose ways in which our very strong intuitions about things such as truth, knowledge, predictions of the future, and rational choices come into conflict. And the deepest paradoxes point to fundamental flaws in our present thinking about such things. It makes sense, then, that as our ideas about fundamental notions such as matter, reality, freedom, space, time, rationality, thought, and other things are called into question, new theories will emerge to better understand these things. And these new theories and understandings

Although the deepest philosophical paradoxes remain unyielding to the many solutions given to them, the solutions themselves have been interesting and useful in their own right.

will lead to more paradoxes. For this reason, new paradoxes are generated as a result of new theories. In these final sections, I will examine the ways in which this happens.

3.4.1 The Science of Paradox Solution

Philosophers Karl Popper, Thomas Kuhn, and Imre Lakatos each give accounts of scientific progress: specifically, how theories, or research programs, replace each other. Paradoxes and solutions figure in each of their accounts in unique ways. By Popper's account, unless they are immediately and conclusively solved, paradoxes that arise from a theory falsify it. For Kuhn, paradoxes and what he calls "puzzles" can peacefully coexist with a scientific theory that gives rise to the paradoxes and puzzles until they begin to multiply and other forces, sometimes sociological ones, begin to call the present paradigm into question. Lakatos, on the other hand, holds that paradoxes can exist and falsify some nonessential elements of a research program but that the core of the program is not open to revision. Only the less essential assumptions made by the program are open to revision in the face of paradoxes and other types of problematic results. Although they are, strictly speaking, not falsified, research programs are either progressing or degenerating based on how many new and correct predictions result.

In addition to being involved in the historical progress of science, the historical progress of solutions to paradoxes might also be examined using the lenses of the Popperian, Kuhnian, and Lakatosian accounts. In doing this, we'll see that nothing even approaching "progress" in the standard sense has occurred for solutions to most paradoxes. Taking this as inductive evidence, I'll conclude that standard paradox solutions using novel theories simply do not work.

3.4.2 The Popperian Account

Popper, like Kuhn and Lakatos, has a view of the progress of science that is markedly different from that of the earlier scientific empiricism. According to this earlier view, scientific progress involves the collection of more and more facts, with one scientific theory incorporating a previous theory into it rather than totally displacing it. Under the scientific empiricist view, progress involves getting more and more newer and more general propositions. One theory does not replace another but rather incorporates the old theory into a more general account. Implicit in this view is the idea that although they are in principle refutable, scientific propositions are rarely overturned by further research.

In *The Logic of Scientific Discovery*, Popper (1959) instead portrays scientific progress as happening by means of a series of "bold conjectures and refutations." The scientist offers a hypothesis and then attempts to refute it. To do this, a consequence of the hypothesis is deduced and then tested. If the empirical evidence supports the consequence, then the hypothesis is not rejected but is not considered "verified," either. It has merely passed one test, and it will be subject to other tests.

As for a paradox that might arise from a scientific theory, Popper has little to say, which is understandable given his focus on empirical evidence. Yet some of the scientific paradoxes rely on the discovery of a surprising conclusion. Consider, for example, something that has been called the *pollution paradox*.

3.4.3 The Pollution Paradox

The *pollution paradox* is a weak paradox, but it is an example of how new sciences lead to further discoveries that cause a reevaluation of the basic notions of the science. The paradox illustrates how intuitions about things such as pollution may be misleading. Normally, industrial pollution is a bad thing. We can see this most obviously in places like Beijing, China, where there is a growing concern about acid rain, greenhouse gas emissions, dust storms set off by drier deserts, and so on. Yet one recent finding made by some scientists in China was that one form of pollution, acid rain, was responsible for cutting down on the levels of another form of pollution, greenhouse gas emissions. In addition to reducing methane, "the sulfate component of acid rain might actually boost rice yields," suggested Dr. Gauci, an author of a study describing the paradox (O'Sullivan 2008). Although one cringes at how such a study might be misused by pollution-generating entities, it does highlight a previously unrecognized interplay between the various elements in our environment and suggest that our previous conception of all industrial pollution as bad might not be completely accurate.

By the Popperian account, the assumption that all pollution has negative effects on the environment has been falsified via the existence of an instance in which this is not the case. It must therefore be rejected. Paradoxes that take the form of assumptions leading to surprising and contradictory results then lead to the falsification of hypotheses.

Popper's is an account that applies to scientific theories. However, with assumptions that lead to paradoxes in other domains—such as truth and the liar, vagueness and the sorites, knowledge and the skeptical paradoxes—applying the Popperian account of paradox leads to a similar conclusion. The assumptions that lead to obvious empirical falsity are therefore falsified. What was taken as obvious truth—for example, that statements are either true or not true—must be wrong. Paradoxes, then, by way of the Popperian account, have thoroughgoing consequences for the assumptions that lead to them.

3.4.4 The Kuhnian Account of Paradox
For Kuhn, the existence of paradox does not necessarily lead to the falsification of the background assumptions that lead to it, any more than the existence of disconfirming

evidence leads to the rejection of a scientific hypothesis. In his famous work *The Structure of Scientific Revolutions*, Kuhn argues that the history of science consists of the adoption and rejection of one scientific paradigm after another. Paradigms, for Kuhn, are "universally recognized scientific achievements that for a long time provide model problems and solutions for a community of practitioners" (1962, x). Paradigms provide not only the theoretical groundwork shared by the scientific community but also the methodological groundwork dictating how further research is to be done. Examples include the Ptolemaic view, which placed the Earth at the center of the universe; Newtonian mechanics, with its laws of motion; Einstein's theory of relativity; the Darwinian theory of natural selection; and quantum mechanics.

According to Kuhn, "The successive transition from one paradigm to another via revolution is the usual developmental pattern of mature science" (1962, 12). Rather than incorporating an earlier theory, a new theory overthrows its predecessor via revolution. Each revolution occurs in stages, beginning with a period of *normal science*, which occurs after a new paradigm has been adopted. During this period, the paradigm is not subject to refutation. The period is one of "puzzle-solving," and puzzles are "that special category of problems that can serve to test ingenuity or skill in solution" (Kuhn 1962, 36). In addition, there are rules provided by the paradigm to "delimit both the nature of acceptable solutions, and the steps by which they are to be obtained" (38). During the period of normal science, any "anomalies" or possible falsifications that arise are dealt with by using auxiliary hypotheses, by ignoring the anomalies, or by suppression. In contrast to Popper, who holds that any falsifications will disprove a theory, Kuhn holds that it is a matter of scientific fact that apparent falsifications do not always lead to disproof. For example, in the period during which Einstein's theory was paradigmatic, certain apparent experimental falsifications were discovered by Miller. These falsifications, however, were not considered to disprove Einstein's theory.

Once the anomalies begin to accumulate, however, and cannot be easily explained away or ignored, the theory enters a period of crisis. During the period of crisis, the theory is no longer capable of supporting the "puzzle-solving traditions" (Kuhn 1962, 67). For example, "The state of Ptolemaic astronomy was a scandal before Copernicus' announcement . . . [and] Galileo's contribution to the study of motion depended closely upon difficulties discovered in Aristotle's theory by Scholastic critics" (67). The period in which the paradigm is in crisis is one characterized by what Kuhn calls "pronounced professional insecurity" (67–68), the result of repeated failures of the puzzles of normal science to be solved.

Following the crisis stage is a period of revolutionary science, characterized by "the proliferation of competing articulations, the willingness to try anything, the expression of explicit discontent, the recourse to philosophy and to debate over the fundamentals" (Kuhn 1962, 91). During this period, different paradigms compete until one is accepted. The factors that determine which paradigm is accepted are often extrascientific. According to Kuhn, the reasons for choosing one paradigm over another are not due to logic and experiment alone. Factors such as the personality and the rhetorical skill of the scientist are often more important than rational grounds for choosing one theory over another. For example, Feyerabend, in his more thoroughgoing critique of the view that theories are chosen on rational grounds, presents a telling example of the "subterfuge, rhetoric, and propaganda" used by Galileo, who used tactics in which "offensive interpretations are replaced by others, propaganda and appeal to distant, and highly theoretic parts of common sense are used to defuse old habits and to enthrone new ones" (Feyerabend 1975, 99).

In addition, Kuhn holds that what is called the "theory informity of observation sentences" precludes any objective, rational evaluation of competing paradigms. For Kuhn, there is no theory-independent observational language. That is, there is no way to observe the physical world without also assuming a theory that describes it. Therefore, there is no fully objective way to adjudicate between scientific theories. However, Kuhn does acknowledge that theories *may* be chosen for their predictive success. A later science is better at problem solving than its predecessors. Einstein's theory, for example, was better at problem solving than Newton's, at least when it came to explaining the movements of very large and very small objects. Of course, one might object that predictive success then is an objective measure by which to adjudicate between theories.

According to Kuhn, no two rival paradigms are compatible because "if new theories are called forth to resolve anomalies in the relation of an existing theory to nature, then the successful new theory must somewhere make predictions that are different from those derived from its predecessor. That difference could not occur if the two were logically compatible" (1962, 97). This account of prediction provides an important objection to the scientific empiricist claim that new theories absorb old ones. If a new theory makes different predictions from an old one, then it seems that one cannot absorb the other. Another feature of rival theories, according to Kuhn, is that they are incommensurable. In other words, one theory will posit the existence of objects different from those posited by another, and the terms they use will not be translatable from one theory to another.

To be a Kuhnian about paradoxes is thus to hold that paradoxes do not lead to great revolutions in science but are pushed to the side in periods of normal science. Only when coupled with extralogical grounds are paradoxes the subject of concern for a theory. Such a view mirrors a good deal the way in which most paradoxes are treated. Although Russell's paradox was thought to have caused Frege to see his previous view as falsified, not many philosophers in general treat the fact that a theory gives rise to a paradox as grounds for rejecting that theory. Indeed, if we think of our folk concepts about truth—vague terms such as bald, knowledge, chance, and so on—as emerging from folk theories, it is hard to see how these folk theories can be rejected by the existence of a paradox, especially without some other equally intuitive notion to be put it in its stead.

The puzzle-solving that occurs in the period of normal science also has implications for attempts to solve paradoxes. Because paradoxes call into question our basic intuitions about folk concepts such as truth and knowledge, concepts not easily replaced, it is natural for the first response to these "puzzles" to be to try to solve them in order to revive faith in the folk theories. If we consider our basic folk theories to be something akin to normal science, then solution-types 1 through 4—which try to decisively do away with the paradox—are seen as the standard ways in which paradoxes are to be "solved."

Another parallel lies in the stage of paradox solution. If we think of solutions as coming from particular Kuhnian stages, the different competing logics in the offing indicate that the science of logic itself is undergoing some kind of revolutionary process. However, no one logic has yet to achieve priority over the others.

3.4.5 A Lakatosian Account of Paradox

For Imre Lakatos, scientific objectivity can be preserved through a more sophisticated form of falsificationism than that of Popper, one that takes into account Kuhn's emphasis on the importance of extrascientific factors in theory choice. According to Lakatos, it is the *research program* that is the object of evaluation and not the theory. A research program consists of a *hard core* or *negative heuristic* and a *protective belt* or *positive heuristic*. The hard core is the body of fundamental theory that is "'irrefutable' by the methodological decision of its protagonists" (1970, 133). For Lakatos, "The negative heuristic of the programme forbids us to direct the *modus tollens* at this 'hard core.' Instead we must use our ingenuity or even invent 'auxiliary hypotheses,' which form a protective belt around this core, and we must redirect *modus tollens* to these" (133). This account has been schematized in figure 4.

Although the hard core cannot be falsified, an entire research program can be objectively evaluated based on whether it is a progressive or degenerating program. It is progressive if its protective belt can accommodate previous anomalies and generate new and successful predictions. And a research program is degenerating if such a program, in accommodating anomalies, generates false predictions or generates no new ones at all. An example of the former for Lakatos would be Marxism, and an example of the latter is Freud's psychoanalytic theory.

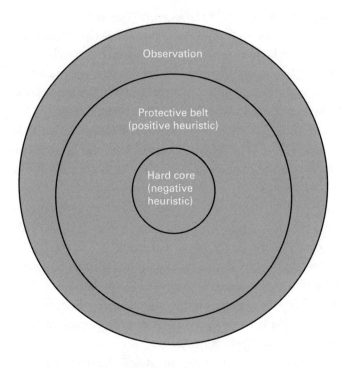

Figure 4 Lakatosian research program

Despite holding that there are objective grounds for determining whether a research program is progressing or degenerating, Lakatos's view differs from Popper's in that Lakatos holds that no "crucial experiments" overthrow a research program. This view also differs from Popper's in its treatment of the Quine/Duhem paradox discussed earlier. The paradox points to the fact that disconfirming evidence never fully refutes a scientific hypothesis. According to Lakatos, "The sophisticated falsificationist allows any part of the body of science to be replaced, but only on the condition that it is replaced in a 'progressive way,' so that the replacement successfully anticipates novel facts" (1970, 187). Any hypothesis can be replaced, as long as the replacements make novel and better predictions.

3.4.6 An Example from Quantum Mechanics: The EPR Paradox

In 1935, when quantum mechanics was fast replacing Albert Einstein's theory of relativity as the dominant physics,[5] Einstein published with Boris Podolsky and Nathan Rosen (1935) an article titled "Can Quantum-Mechanical Description of Physical Reality Be Considered Complete?" In this piece, they presented a case in which assumptions made by quantum mechanics led to strongly counterintuitive results. The argument showing the counterintuitive consequences was dubbed the *Einstein-Podolsky-Rosen paradox* or the *EPR paradox*.

It was already known at the time that there was some uncertainty about measuring objects on the quantum level. For example, it was known that the outcome of predicting where every photon (smallest quantity of light) would go if a beam of light were directed toward a half-silvered mirror (i.e., with one half shiny side) and then reduced until one photon at a time was hitting the mirror is uncertain. Some of the photons will be reflected back and others will not, and determining each and every photon's path cannot be done. To account for this, Heisenberg's uncertainty principle was used. According to this principle, every physical quantity has what are called *conjugate properties*. An example of a pair of conjugate properties is momentum and position. Heisenberg claimed that if you measure the position of a particle, then the momentum is indeterminate. And if you measure the momentum, the position is indeterminate. The EPR paradox (figure 5) shows that this explanation is insufficient. It did so by taking two entangled particles, A and B, and showing that when one conjugate property of A was measured—say, the location—the other conjugate property of B, the momentum, was rendered indeterminate. And this happened even if A and B were not in direct contact with each other. From this, Einstein and colleagues inferred that either the two particles were interacting in some way, though they were separated, or else the information about all the possible outcomes was already in the particles, encoded in some "hidden parameters."

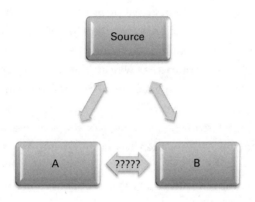

Figure 5 EPR paradox

The proposers of the paradox believed that the latter was the case, because the instantaneous interaction, across a distance, of distinct particles was not only supremely counterintuitive but also violated Einstein's principle of relativity, which held that nothing travels faster than the speed of light. A standard interpretation of quantum mechanics, the Copenhagen interpretation, though, assumed no "hidden variables" and assumed that the properties in a physical system do not exist prior to their measurement. So, although one response to EPR is to hold that there is some hidden variable influencing the two systems, another rejects the idea that we can meaningfully refer to objects and their properties prior to their measurement. The Copenhagen interpretation, in rejecting what is called *local realism*—the view that objects/properties exist in a definite state independently of their being measured—also rejects the idea that we can speak meaningfully of the definiteness of results that have not yet been measured.

To put EPR in standard form, let's start with the definition of *paradox* as *a set of mutually inconsistent propositions, each of which seems true*:

Box 23

EPR paradox

1. The principles of quantum mechanics provide the most complete and most accurate account of the nature of physical reality.
2. It follows from the principles of quantum mechanics that two quantities may instantaneously influence each other, without there being contact between them.

The first statement was then and is now still believed true by most physicists. The second statement was demonstrably shown by Einstein, Podolsky, and Rosen and is hardly subject to doubt. How can these two statements be reconciled? Einstein and colleagues thought that the easiest solution was to reject the first statement—in particular, the view that quantum mechanics is complete—and admit that much work still needed to be done before considering it the paradigmatic physics. Indeed, Einstein spent the rest of his life attempting to do this, without success (Moore 1966). However, this was not how the general scientific community reacted to the EPR paradox. Instead, physicists focused on what they called the *principle of locality*, which is the view that something that happens in one location can have no *immediate* effect on something at another location, and something called *local realism*, the view that the properties of objects must have a preexisting value before they are measured. For example, local realism assumes that an object must have a preexisting location before the location of the object is measured. Both the principle of locality and local realism are highly intuitive. The principle of locality states that if there is to be an effect, it must not be instantaneous but must happen afterward. In other words, causes must precede their effects, by however miniscule a period of time. This rule is basic intuition about causality. If A causes B, then it seems that A must happen at least a little time before B. And local realism, as Einstein famously said, embodies the intuition that "the moon is there even if I'm not looking at it" (Bernstein 2007).

Instead of taking the EPR as falsifying the core ideas of quantum mechanics, though, the principle of locality and local realism—less central tenets, ones in the "protective belt" of the research program— were ultimately called into question. On certain interpretations of quantum mechanics, such as the Copenhagen interpretation, these were to be rejected. Debates about the EPR, and how to best deal with it, are ongoing among physicists. Should we consider quantum mechanics a progressive or degenerating research program? If predictive success and practical applications are any indication, then quantum mechanics—with its ability to predict the movements of the smallest particles in the universe and having given rise to major applications such as transistors, integrated circuits, and lasers—is still a progressive research program.

As we have seen, paradoxes under the Lakatosian view do not have the wholesale consequences that the Popperian account implies. A theory that gives rise to a paradox is not falsified. In response to the paradox, certain auxiliary assumptions made by the theory can be replaced as long as the revisions lead to new and better predictions. We can see this at work in the Detour solution-type.

3.5   The Moral from Theories of Scientific Progress for Solutions to Paradoxes

If we hold Popper's basic falsificationism, paradoxes falsify theories. If we accept Kuhn's relativism/reliance on predictive success, paradoxes can be ignored or treated as "puzzles" to be solved in a period of normal science. When science enters crisis, however, the paradoxes become more damning and there is a struggle for different theories to provide accounts that solve or sidestep them. And if we accept Lakatos' variant of falsificationism, paradoxes give rise to the changes in the protective belt of a research program, given that successful novel predictions are generated. Each of these approaches to paradoxes presents a case against the view that paradoxes get decisively solved by solution-types 1 through 4. For the Popperian falsificationist, paradoxes simply refute theories. Their existence, without any immediate and decisive solutions, shows that the background folk theories from which paradoxes arise are flawed. Such folk theories are to be rejected if paradoxes are to be avoided. However, folk theories are there for a reason, a cognitive one, and hence cannot be rejected so easily. For the Kuhnian relativist, a survey through the history of solutions to paradoxes, with its limited successes, indicates either that the theories that attempt to provide solutions to them are in a prescientific stage or that an ongoing state of revolution is occurring with no obvious winner to be chosen as a new paradigm. And, taking a Lakatosian view, we are left to conclude that treating the history of solutions to paradoxes in a similar way as the history of science shows that, in general, paradox solution in its standard sense of an approach involving solution-types 1 through 4, is a degenerating research program.

Whatever lens through which we view the progress of paradox solution, the most rational conclusion to make is that not much in the way of progress has occurred for solutions to the deepest paradoxes.

CONCLUSION

There are many reasons why philosophers study philosophical paradoxes. Paradoxes force those who study and attempt to solve them to confront strong, conflicting intuitions; discover ways in which intuitions can be misleading; and analyze ways in which our ordinary concepts are problematic. In addition, paradoxes require the adventurous souls who seek to understand and solve them to go beyond a noncommittal awareness of philosophical problems to an evaluation of solutions that are—to varying degrees—successful. And most important, students of paradoxes learn that discovering a paradox—ironically—leads to advances in our knowledge, not the reverse. As scientist Niels Bohr wrote, "How wonderful that we have met with a paradox. Now we have some hope of making progress" (Moore 1966, 196). The contemporary solutions to the paradoxes we have met in this book show the wisdom of Bohr's statement. Not only are the solutions to the paradoxes original and interesting, but the systematic theories here highlighted are interesting in their own right and have led to much progress in the way we think about a wide array of notions, whether in science, mathematics, politics, or philosophy. Where there is progress, there is paradox. Each fuels the other.

GLOSSARY

Argument
A piece of reasoning in which one statement (the conclusion) is supported by other statements (the premises).

Axiom
A statement that is assumed to be true without proof.

Conclusion
A statement in an argument that is supported by premises.

Deductive argument
An argument in which the conclusion is presented as following with necessity from the premises.

Fallacy
An error in reasoning.

Fuzzy logic
A type of logic that rejects the classical two values T and F and replaces them with unit intervals.

Inductive argument
An argument in which the conclusion is presented as following with a high probability from the premises.

Intuition
What seems to be the case; noninferential belief; what we would say in a given situation.

Logic
The study of the methods and principles for distinguishing good reasoning from bad.

Paradox
A set of mutually inconsistent propositions, each of which seems true; an argument with seemingly true premises, seemingly good reasoning, and an obviously false or contradictory conclusion; an unacceptable conclusion derived from seemingly true premises and apparently valid reasoning.

Premise
A statement offered in support of a conclusion.

Soundness
A deductive argument is sound when its premises are true and the argument is valid.

Syllogism
A two-premise deductive argument that employs three main terms major, minor, and middle. The major term is the predicate term of the conclusion. The minor term is the subject term of the conclusion. The middle term occurs in each premise but not the conclusion. For example, consider the following deductive argument:

1. All men are mortal.
2. Socrates is a man.
3. Socrates is mortal.

Mortal is the major term, *man* is the middle term, and *Socrates* is the minor term. Every syllogism has a major premise that contains the major term and a minor premise that contains the minor term. In this case, (1) is the major premise and (2) is the minor premise.

Subjective probability
The degree to which one believes something.

Validity
A deductive argument is valid when it is impossible for its premises to be true and its conclusion false; in a valid deductive argument, the premises fully support the conclusion.

NOTES

Introduction
1. Here someone might object that the no-smoking ashtray example does not contain premises and a conclusion, so reasoning is not central to what a paradox is. I'd respond that in the case of the ashtray, the self-flowing flask, and so on, the "facts" related to these items can be turned into statements, and pieces of reasoning be constructed out of them. For example, the ashtray paradox can be put as follows: (1) it is hereby ordered that you not smoke, (2) it is hereby ordered that when you smoke, you use this ashtray, (3) therefore, it is hereby ordered that you smoke (from 2) and not smoke (from 1).

1 A New Way to Think about Paradoxes and Solutions
1. Admittedly, this is not a very deep paradox, given that although it is surprising, there is nothing inconsistent with granting the conclusion, given the assumption.
2. This is, admittedly, a very simplistic account of combined subjective probability, but it works for our purposes. If this were to be fleshed out to account cases in which A and B are dependent on each other, then the combined probability of A and B should be the probability of A multiplied by the probability of B given A (i.e., $P(A \& B) = P(A) \times P(B \mid A)$). In the vast majority of cases, though, a simple multiplication of A and B is fine.
3. See the glossary for a definition of *validity*. For simplicity, you can think of valid reasoning here as "good" reasoning.

2 How to Solve Paradoxes
1. Usually, another axiom is added that wasn't original to ZF—the axiom of choice—and the theory is abbreviated ZFC.
2. An axiom schema differs from an axiom in that it contains one or more variables as placeholders for a term of subformula of the language.
3. It is given that A and H entail e, but not-e is observed. Also the probability of observing not-e while A and H are true is 0. That is, $P(\text{not-e} \mid A \text{ and } H) = 0$.

   We assigned H a very high probability, $P(H) = 0.9$, whereas we have assigned A a prior probability that makes it only slightly more likely than not: $P(A) = 0.6$. We also assumed that H and A are statistically independent. That is, the probability of H does not change the probability of A, or vice versa.

With regard to the assumed likelihoods, the probability of not-e being observed, given that A is true and not-H is assumed to be a very small number, x (for example, 0.001). That is, P(not-e | A and not-H) = x. On the other hand, we assumed the likelihood of not-e being observed given not-A being the case is assumed to be 50 times more likely, 50x. So: P(not-e | not-A and not-H) = 50x and P (not-e | not-A and H) = 50x.

We then plug these numbers into a form of Bayes' theorem:

P(H | not-e) = P(not-e | H) P(H)
P(not-e)

P(not-e) = P(not-e | H) P(H) + P(not-e | not-H) P(not-H)

P(not-e | H) = P(not-e | A and H) P(A) + P(not-e | not-A and H) P(not-A)

= 0 + 50x (0.4)

= 20.6x

P(not-e) = 20x (0.9) + 2.06x = 20.06x.

For the posterior probability of H,

$$P(H \mid \text{not-e}) = \frac{20x(0.9)}{20.06x} = 0.897$$

For the posterior probability of A,

P(A | not-e) = P(not-e | A) P (A)
P(not-e)

P(not-e | A) = P(not-e | A and H) P(H) + P(not-e | A and not-H) P(not-H)

= 0 + x (0.1) = 0.1x

$$P(A \mid \text{not-e}) = \frac{0.06x}{20.06x} = 0.003$$

Whereas the probability of H is hardly changed, the probability of A plummets.

4. Here you might notice that the way of determining truth-values for conjunctions in fuzzy logic is different from the simple multiplication used in determining the combined subjective probabilities in our discussion of the paradoxicality rating in chapter 1. According to fuzzy logic, a low truth-value of say, 0.2, when combined with one of say, 0.9, will result in a combined truth value of 0.2, and the subjective probability as we are determining it will be 0.18—only slightly lower. But for 0.4 and 0.5 values, the combined truth-value on fuzzy logic is 0.4, while the combined subjective probability of the two, if these values are taken for degrees of belief, will be 0.2—less than half than that of taking the minimum of the two values. For us, using the straightforward multiplication makes sense because we want a greatly reduced degree of belief for even a little bit of uncertainty. When dealing with degrees of truth, on the other hand, this approach is not necessary, or even desirable.

3   Paradox Lost? On the Successes (and Failures) of Solutions to Paradoxes

1. For Schiffer, a *happy-face* solution points to a flawed part of the paradox, and then explains why we mistakenly believed that the flaw was acceptable.

2. A discussion of the puzzles associated with comparing infinite sets, for example, was given by Albert of Saxony (1492) in his *Questiones subtilissime in libros de cello et mundo*.

3. I am not an historian of logic, but I am interested the history of solutions. There are interesting connections to more recent solutions, and these solutions provide inductive grounds for drawing a generalization about solutions to paradoxes. A prime resource I used was Kneale and Kneale 1962.

4. Stephen Read (2002) has a somewhat different, and much fuller, take on this.

5. These theories deal with different types of phenomena and are not, strictly speaking, in conflict. However, one emerged as more prominent than the other.

REFERENCES

Albert of Saxony. 1492. *Questiones Subtilissime in Libros de Celo et Mundo*. http://echo.mpiwgberlin.mpg.de/ECHOdocuView?url=/permanent/library/0PUX1P29/index.meta&pn=1.

Aristotle. 350 BCE. *Sophistical Refutations*. http://classics.mit.edu/Aristotle/sophist_refut.html.

Aristotle. 350 BCE. *Physics*. http://classics.mit.edu/Aristotle/physics.html.

Bernstein, Jeremy. 2007. Einstein: An Exchange. *New York Review of Books*. http://www.nybooks.com/articles/archives/2007/aug/16/einstein-an-exchange/?pagination=false.

Burns, Linda. 1991. *Vagueness: An Investigation into Natural Languages and the Sorites Paradox*. Dordrecht: Kluwer.

Clark, Michael. 2007. *Paradoxes from A to Z*. New York: Routledge.

Davis-Floyd, R., and P. S. Arvidson, eds. 1997. *Intuition: The Inside Story*. New York: Routledge.

Duhem, Pierre. 1954. *Essays in the History and Philosophy of Science*. Trans. P. Barker and R. Ariew. Indianapolis: Hackett.

Dummett, Michael. 1975. Wang's Paradox. *Synthese* 30:301–324.

Einstein, Albert, Boris Podolsky, and Nathan Rosen. 1935. Can Quantum-Mechanical Description of Physical Reality Be Considered Complete? *Physical Review* 41:777. http://www.nat.vu.nl/~wimu/Pictures/EPR-paper.pdf.

Feyerabend, Paul 1975. *Against Method*. New York: New Left Books.

Fine, Kit. 1975. Vagueness, Truth and Logic. *Synthese* 30:265–300.

Flugel, J. C. 1941. "The Moral Paradox of Peace and War." Conway Memorial Lecture. London: Watts and Company.

Hume, David. 1757. Of the Standard of Taste. Ed. Jonathan Bennett, 7–19. http://www.earlymoderntexts.com/pdfbits/htaste.pdf.

James, William. 1906/2008. *Pragmatism: A New Name for Some Old Ways of Thinking*. Rockville, MD: Arc Manor.

Jeffrey, Richard. 2004. *Subjective Probability*. New York: Cambridge University Press.

Kahneman, Daniel. 2011. *Thinking, Fast and Slow*. New York: Farrar, Straus, and Giroux.

Kant, Immanuel. 1969. *Critique of Pure Reason*. Trans. Norman Kemp-Smith. New York: St. Martin's Press.

Kneale, Willam, and Martha Kneale. 1962. *The Development of Logic*. New York: Oxford University Press.

Kripke, Saul. 1975. Outlines of a Theory of Truth. *Journal of Philosophy* 72:690–716.

Kuhn, Thomas. 1962. *The Structure of Scientific Revolutions*. Chicago: University of Chicago Press. http://www.f.waseda.jp/sidoli/Kuhn_Structure_of_Scientific_Revolutions.pdf.

Lakatos, Imre. 1970. Falsification and the Methodology of Scientific Research Programmes. In *Criticism and the Growth of Knowledge*, ed. Imre Lakatos and Alan Musgrave, 170–196. New York: Cambridge University Press.

Laudan, Larry. 1977. *Progress and Its Problems*. London: Routledge.

Lee, H. D. P. 1967. *Zeno of Elea: A Text with Translation and Notes*. Amsterdam: Hakkert.

MacDonald, Alistair. 2011. "Honestly, This Part of England Has the World's Biggest Liars." *Wall Street Journal*, November 25.

Machina, Kenton. 1976. Truth, Belief, and Vagueness. *Journal of Philosophical Logic* 5 (1): 47–78.

Mackie, J. L. 1973. *Truth, Probability, and Paradox*. New York: Oxford University Press.

May, Robert. 1972. Limit Cycles in Predator-Prey Communities. *Science* 177 (492): 900–902.

Mayo, Deborah. 1997. Duhem's Problem, the Bayesian Way, and Error Statistics: What's Belief Got to Do with It? *Philosophy of Science* 64:222–244.

Moaz, Zeev. 1990. *Paradoxes of War*. Boston: Unwin Hyman.

Moore, Ruth. 1966. *Niels Bohr: The Man, His Science, and the World They Changed*. New York: Knopf.

O'Neill, Barry. 1986. International Escalation and the Dollar Cost Auction. *Journal of Conflict Resolution* 30:33–50.

O'Sullivan, Marion. 2008. Acid Rain Reduces Methane Emissions from Rice Paddies. *Innovations Report*, August 7. http://www.innovations-report.de/html/berichte/umwelt_naturschutz/acid_rain_reduces_methane_emissions_rice_paddies_115639.html.

Parikh, Rohit. 1994. Vagueness and Utility. *Linguistics and Philosophy* 17 (6): 521–535.

Plato. 2005. *Parmenides*. In *The Collected Dialogues of Plato*, ed. Edith Hamilton and Huntington Cairns, 920–996. Princeton: Princeton University Press.

Read, Stephen. 2002. The Liar Paradox from John Buridan Back to Thomas Bradwardine. *Vivarium*. http://academia.edu/1353385/The_liar_paradox_from_John_Buridan_back_to_Thomas_Bradwardine.

Rescher, Nicholas. 2001. *Paradoxes: Their Roots, Range, and Resolution*. Chicago: OpenCourt.

Rosenzweig, Michael. 1971. The Paradox of Enrichment. *Science* 171: 385–387.

Sainsbury, R. M. 2009. *Paradoxes*. 3rd ed. Cambridge: Cambridge University Press.

Schiffer, Stephen. 1996. Contextualist Solutions to Skepticism. *Proceedings of the Aristotelian Society* 96:317–333.

Schiffer, Stephen. 1999. Two Issues of Vagueness. *Monist* 81 (2): 193–214.

Schiffer, Stephen. 2003. *The Things We Mean*. New York: Oxford University Press.

Spade, Paul Vincent. 1988. *Lies, Language, and Logic in the Later Middle Ages*. London: Variorum.

Spade, Paul Vincent. 2009. Insolubles. In *Stanford Encyclopedia of Philosophy*. http://plato.stanford.edu/entries/insolubles/.

Tarán, Leonardo. 1965. *Parmenides*. Princeton: Princeton University Press.

Tarski, Alfred. 1944. The Semantic Conception of Truth and the Foundations of Semantics. *Philosophy and Phenomenological Research* 4:341–375.

van Fraassen, Bas. 1966. Singular Terms, Truth-Value Gaps, and Free Logic. *Journal of Philosophy* 63 (17): 481–495.

van Heijenoort, Jean. 1967. *From Frege to Godel: A Source Book in Mathematical Logic, 1879–1931*. Cambridge, MA: Harvard University Press.

Watson, J. B. 1930. *Behaviourism*. Chicago: University of Chicago Press.

Williamson, Timothy. 1994. *Vagueness*. New York: Routledge.

FURTHER READINGS

BBC. 2010. *Paradox* (television series). Season 1.

Bell, J. 1964. On the Einstein Podolsky Rosen Paradox. *Physics* 1 (3): 195–200.

Chihara, Charles. 1979. The Semantic Paradoxes. *Philosophical Review* 88 (4): 590–618.

Hume, David. 1757. "Of the Standard of Taste." http://academic.evergreen. edu/curricular/IBES/files/taste_hume.pdf.

Jeffrey, Richard. 2004. *Subjective Probability*. New York: Cambridge University Press.

Mayo, Deborah. 1996. *Error and the Growth of Experimental Knowledge*. Chicago: University of Chicago Press.

McNeill, Daniel, and Paul Freiberger. 1993. *Fuzzy Logic*. New York: Simon and Schuster.

Salmon, Wesley. 2001. *Zeno's Paradoxes*. Indianapolis: Hackett.

Steinhart, Eric. 2009. *More Precisely: The Math You Need to Do Philosophy*. Toronto: Broadview Press.

INDEX

MARGARET CUONZO is Associate Professor of Philosophy and Coordinator of Humanities at Long Island University, Brooklyn.